P9-DEY-760

3 1611 00000 4314

UNIVERSITY PARK
IL 60466

WITHDRAWN

Also by Barry Denenberg:

The True Story of J. Edgar Hoover
and the FBI

. . .

Nelson Mandela:
"No Easy Walk to Freedom"

. . .

Stealing Home:
The Story of Jackie Robinson

. . .

John Fitzgerald Kennedy:
America's 35th President

VOICES *from* VIETNAM

GOVERNORS STATE UNIVERSITY
UNIVERSITY PARK
IL 60466

VOICES *from* VIETNAM

· · ·

barry Denenberg

SCHOLASTIC
HARDCOVER

SCHOLASTIC INC. · NEW YORK

MAT-CTR. DS 559.5 .D46 1995

Denenberg, Barry.

Voices from Vietnam

314 546

Copyright © 1995 by Barry Denenberg.
All rights reserved. Published by Scholastic Inc.
SCHOLASTIC HARDCOVER is a registered trademark of Scholastic Inc.

No part of this publication may be reproduced in whole or in part, or stored in a
retrieval system, or transmitted in any form or by any means, electronic, mechani-
cal, photocopying, recording, or otherwise, without written permission of the
publisher. For information regarding permission, write to Scholastic Inc.,
555 Broadway, New York, NY 10012.

LIBRARY OF CONGRESS CATALOGING-IN-PUBLICATION DATA
Denenberg, Barry. Voices from Vietnam / Barry Denenberg.
p. cm. Includes bibliographical references.

ISBN 0-590-44267-8

1. Vietnamese Conflict. 1961–1975—Personal narratives—Juvenile literature.
[1. Vietnamese Conflict, 1961–1975—Personal narratives.] I. Title.
DS559.5.D46 1994   959.704' 38—dc20   93-44886 CIP AC

12 11 10 9 8 7 6 5 4 3 2 1   5 6 7 8 9 /9 0/0

Printed in the U.S.A.   23
First printing, January 1995
Designed by Michele Chism

Contents

. . .

Introduction

The Vietnam War was the longest war in American history, although war was never declared. Like the Civil War, the nation was bitterly divided by it. It is the first war the United States ever lost.

There are a number of books that tell the historical origins of the war and the political decision making that shaped its course. This book is not about the politics or history of the Vietnam War.

It is about what it was like to be in Vietnam. More than two and a half million American men and women served there. More than three hundred thousand of them were wounded — one hundred and fifty thousand seriously. Untold thousands more were damaged psychologically — some permanently. Fifty-eight thousand Americans died there.

Voices from Vietnam is about them. Their stories told, largely, in their own words. It is to them that it is dedicated.

It still boils down to suffering, and the thing
about Vietnam that most bothers me is that
it is treated as a political experience, a sociological
experience, and the human element of what a
soldier goes through—and what the Vietnamese went
through—is not only neglected: it is almost cast
aside as superfluous.
                              —Tim O'Brien, U.S. Army

"Sure rains a lot here . . ."

APO 96225

A young man once went off to war
in a far country
When he had time, he wrote home and
said, "Sure rains here a lot."

But his mother, reading between the lines,
Wrote, "We're quite concerned. Tell us
what it's really like."

And the young man responded, "Wow, you ought
to see the funny monkeys!"

To which the mother replied, "Don't
hold back, how is it?"

And the young man wrote, "The sunsets here
are spectacular."

In her next letter the mother
wrote, "Son we want you to tell us
everything."

So the next time he wrote,
"Today I killed a man.
Yesterday I helped drop napalm on women and
children. Tomorrow we are going to use
gas."

And the father wrote, "Please don't
write such depressing letters. You're upsetting
your mother."

So, after a while, the young man wrote, "Sure rains a
lot here..."

                              Larry Rottmann, U.S. Army

VOICES *from* VIETNAM

Part One

The quagmire

. . .

1945–1963

Chapter One

the · dirty · war

I WANTED TO GO SEE. . .THE PEOPLE. . .AS I
WENT AROUND, I WAS IMPRESSED WITH THE BASIC
HATRED FOR THE FRENCH.

— ABBOT LOW MOFFAT, U.S. DEPARTMENT OF STATE

· · ·

WE LEARNED . . . ABOUT THE STRUGGLE AGAINST THE
FRENCH. . . . WE WERE TAUGHT HOW BRUTAL THE
FRENCH HAD BEEN, HOW THEY ENSLAVED VIETNAM. WE
LOOKED AT PICTURES OF WHAT THE FRENCH HAD DONE
— ROWS OF VIETNAMESE SHACKLED IN STOCKS, HEADS
OF MURDERED VIETNAMESE PATRIOTS DISPLAYED BY
FRENCH SOLDIERS. WE READ BIOGRAPHIES AND
MEMOIRS OF MILITANTS WHO HAD DIED UNDER FRENCH
TORTURE OR HAD SPENT YEARS IN JAIL. . . .

— LE THANH, NORTH VIETNAMESE CIVILIAN

· · ·

THE VIETNAMESE HAVE A LONG HISTORY, MUCH OF IT SPENT fighting to remain independent of foreign conquerors. For centuries Vietnam was ruled by China. Then, in the mid-1800's, France seized control and made Vietnam one of its colonies. The French wanted to use Vietnam's raw materials and exploit the local population. Most Vietnamese, especially the peasants, suffered under French rule.

In 1945, after the end of World War II, Vietnamese resistance intensified and grew into a revolt, led by Ho Chi Minh, a Vietnamese communist. The French, however, did not take Ho Chi Minh's army seriously. They called it "the barefoot army." The French, well equipped and well trained, were able to control the cities. But "the barefoot army" was able to gain control of the countryside, where eighty-five percent of the population lived.

Back home, in France, the war had grown unpopular. It had dragged on longer than expected. The French called it "the dirty war." On May 7, 1954, the Vietnamese communists defeated the French in a decisive battle near the village of Dienbienphu, ending "the dirty war."

By that time American money had been paying for nearly eighty percent of the cost of the French war in Vietnam. Now, with France's defeat at Dienbienphu, the United States prepared to take its place.

Chapter Two

the · miracle · man

SHIT, DIEM'S THE ONLY BOY WE GOT OUT THERE.

— VICE-PRESIDENT LYNDON BAINES JOHNSON

PRESIDENT DWIGHT D. EISENHOWER BELIEVED, AS PRESIDENT Truman had before him, that Vietnam must not be allowed to become a communist country. Unless America maintained a powerful presence in the region, the Soviet Union and China could extend their influence throughout Southeast Asia. Eisenhower was determined not to let these small countries fall to the communists.

· · ·

You have a row of dominoes set up, and you knock over the first one and what will happen to the last one is the certainty that it will go over very quickly. So you have the beginning of a disintegration that will have the most profound influences.

— PRESIDENT DWIGHT D. EISENHOWER

· · ·

Two months after the fall of Dienbienphu, the Vietminh and the French signed a cease-fire agreement. The cease-fire was one of the provisions called for by an international conference held in Geneva, Switzerland. The conference had been called to solve cold war problems, including Vietnam. The United States, France, Great Britain, China, the Soviet Union, and representatives of North and South Vietnam were among the nine delegations attending the two-and-a-half-month-long meeting.

The delegates to Geneva recommended that nationwide elections be held in 1956 and that Vietnam be temporarily divided at the 17th parallel. The North would be ruled by Ho Chi Minh's communists and the South by the recently formed government of Ngo Dinh Diem.

President Eisenhower backed the anticommunist Diem and praised him as a "miracle man." The United States supported him with money and materiel.

• • •

The Central Intelligence Agency was given the mission of helping Diem develop a government that would be sufficiently strong and viable to compete with and, if necessary, stand up to the Communist regime of Ho Chi Minh in the north.

— CHESTER COOPER, CENTRAL INTELLIGENCE AGENCY

• • •

Diem was suspicious, eccentric, and arrogant.

• • •

. . . Once Diem started talking, it was impossible to change the subject, or even to attract his attention.

...A mere two-hour session with Diem was considered a "quickie." An ashen-faced American newsman came directly to my office from the palace one day to report that Diem had kept him for six and one-half hours ... with no lunch, and that the last ninety minutes had been spent standing in the doorway after the newsman had gotten up to try to leave.

— JOHN MECKLIN, AMERICAN EMBASSY, SAIGON

•   •   •

Because of his privileged background, Diem had little sympathy for the common Vietnamese peasant who lived in the small villages and hamlets.

Soon after taking office Diem announced that he would not allow nationwide elections intended to unite the country to take place. His government, he said, was too new and therefore too weak. He ignored repeated requests from Ho Chi Minh that the elections be held.

Diem's government proved to be dictatorial, not democratic. He consolidated power in the hands of his family: Three of his brothers held important positions in the government. The most powerful was his ruthless and corrupt brother Ngo Dinh Nhu. Nhu used a secret police force to repress any opposition. His wife, Madame Nhu, became an outspoken and controversial member of the government in her own right.

•   •   •

(She) would tell American officers straight to their faces that her government did not like Americans but it liked having our money.

— JAN BARRY, U.S. ARMY

. . .

By 1958 there were 40,000 political prisoners in South Vietnamese jails. Twelve thousand others had been killed. New laws allowed military courts to execute anyone suspected of disloyalty to the Diem government within three days of their arrest. Mere suspicion was grounds for arrest, and there was no appealing the sentence.

Diem grew even more isolated from the people he was supposed to represent. He became increasingly unpopular as he continued to rule South Vietnam more like an emperor than a president.

. . .

Though Diem had established his own patriotism in years past, he had never been actively engaged in the French war and had spent the last four years of it outside Vietnam. As a result, he viewed the resistance veterans as rivals for power who had to be crushed. Labeling all of them communist or pro-communist, he was using the secret police...to hunt down these people — people who were considered by almost everyone else as freedom fighters.

Watching the political evolution of my country, I saw that the Diem government had many fundamental errors: First, it was a government of one family. Second, Diem suppressed many patriots who participated in the war against the French. Third, he put the Christian religion above the interest of the nation ... eighty percent of the Vietnamese population are Confucian or Buddhists.

— TRUONG NHU TANG, VIETCONG

. . .

8

Chapter Three

bear · any · burden

LET EVERY NATION KNOW, WHETHER IT WISHES US WELL OR
ILL, THAT WE SHALL PAY ANY PRICE, BEAR ANY BURDEN, MEET
ANY HARDSHIP, SUPPORT ANY FRIEND, OPPOSE ANY FOE TO
ASSURE THE SURVIVAL AND SUCCESS OF LIBERTY.
— PRESIDENT JOHN F. KENNEDY

OUR IDEA OF VIETNAM WAS THIS: THIS IS A NEW NATION BEING
BORN. IT HAS TO BE SOMETHING. AND NATURALLY, WE AMERICANS
WERE CONVINCED THAT THE "SOMETHING" SHOULD BE OUR SYSTEM
OF REPRESENTATIVE GOVERNMENT, THE BEST IN THE WORLD. WE
HAD THE SENSE OF MISSION. WE WERE THE NATION THAT HAD
WON WORLD WAR II AND WAS HONORED THROUGHOUT THE
WORLD. . . . WE HAD ENORMOUS PRESTIGE IN THAT PERIOD. . . .
AND VIETNAM WAS AN IDEAL PLACE. IT WAS ENORMOUSLY
ATTRACTIVE IN THOSE DAYS. . . . THERE WAS THAT SENSE
OF A YOUNG COUNTRY, WHICH WAS VERY INSPIRING. IT WAS
A SMALL COUNTRY WHICH MEANT YOU COULD IDENTIFY WITH
IT AS A PROJECT. THERE WAS A VERY GRACEFUL, TRADITIONAL
CULTURE, AN ENORMOUSLY PLEASANT WAY OF LIFE. SAIGON
WAS AN ELEGANT CITY. THE BEAUTIFUL TROPICAL FOLIAGE,
THE FLAMBOYANT TREES. . . . THE WHOLE THING WAS JUST

ELEGANT AND ROMANTIC AS HELL. IT WAS A DREAM COUNTRY
IF YOU LEFT IT ALONE. . . .
IN THOSE DAYS, WHEN YOU HAD U.S. MILITARY ADVISORS
AND THAT'S ALL, NO COMBAT TROOPS. . . . THEY WERE HELPING
TO BUILD A LITTLE PROFESSIONAL ARMY WHICH HAD A MISSION
AGAINST A RUTHLESS, CRUEL, DETERMINED, WELL-ORGANIZED
ENEMY. . . . IT WAS QUITE CLEAR THAT THERE WERE GOOD GUYS
AND BAD GUYS. AND THE GOOD GUYS NEEDED HELP.

— OGDEN WILLIAMS,
CENTRAL INTELLIGENCE AGENCY

IN JANUARY 1961, WHEN JOHN F. KENNEDY WAS INAUGU-
rated president, few Americans had heard of Vietnam.
But the U.S. military presence there had grown and would
continue to grow. During the thousand days of Kennedy's
presidency, the flow of American civilian and military personnel, money, materiel, and weapons increased dramati-
cally. The number of military advisors swelled from 700 to
12,000. More than 2,000 were in the U.S. Special Forces —
the Green Berets, as they were called.

The Green Berets

President Kennedy wanted to avoid sending regular
ground troops into South Vietnam. But he believed that
the country was being disrupted by rebel forces encouraged and supported by the Soviet Union and China. Some
military response was necessary. The new president believed that an unconventional soldier was needed to fight
this "new type of war."

•   •   •

I know that many of you may feel, and many of our citizens may feel, that in these days of the nuclear age, when war may last in its final form a day or two or three days before much of the world is burned up, your service to your country will be only standing and waiting. Nothing, of course, could be further from the truth.

— war by ambush instead of by combat, by infiltration instead of by aggression, seeking victory by eroding and exhausting the enemy instead of engaging him. . . . These are the kinds of challenges that will be before us in the next decade if freedom is to be saved, a whole new kind of strategy, a wholly different kind of force, and therefore a new and wholly different kind of military training.

— PRESIDENT KENNEDY

.   .   .

The president revitalized the U.S. Special Forces, which had first been organized in 1952. He increased the number of the Green Berets (as they came to be called because of their distinctive hats) from 2,500 to 10,000 men.

.   .   .

The President directed — again over the opposition of top generals — that the Special Forces wear green berets as a mark of distinction. He wanted them to be a dedicated, high-quality elite corps of specialists, trained to train local partisans in guerrilla warfare, prepared to perform a wide range of civilian as well as military tasks, able to live off the bush, in a village or behind enemy lines. He personally supervised the selection of new equipment — the replacement of heavy, noisy combat boots with sneakers, for example, and, when the sneakers proved vulnerable to bamboo spikes, their reinforcement with flexible steel inner soles. . . .

— THEODORE SORENSEN, ASSISTANT TO
PRESIDENT KENNEDY

• • •

During the Kennedy years, the American presence in Vietnam was viewed by many as a necessary step to halt the spread of communism, and the Green Berets were to be one weapon in this struggle. The Green Berets were looked upon as a daring and dangerous elite group. They wore, it appeared, whatever they chose, including tiger-striped fatigues, scarves, and native beads. They seemed undisciplined not only in appearance but in behavior. They obeyed military protocol only when it suited them.

The Green Berets were regarded as heroes for a time. In 1966, "The Ballad of the Green Berets," sung by Barry Sadler, became a major, national hit. John Wayne, then a big box-office attraction, starred in a movie about their exploits.

• • •

One has to recall the rhetoric of the Kennedy era. . . . There were notions of patriotism, of serving one's country. . . . It was always a very special relationship between Kennedy and the Special Forces.

— BRIAN JENKINS, U.S. ARMY SPECIAL FORCES

• • •

... at the beginning ... of the war, the Green Berets were a symbol of counterinsurgency and they were excellent. What happened was that they — Barry Sadler was the worst thing that ever happened to them. He came out with this song and all of a sudden the Green Berets no more were an elite small unit. They got all kinds of cowboys in there, and the cowboys wanted to go out and shoot and kick down doors and beat up people. That's not the way to run a counter-guerrilla outfit. You don't win any friends by going into a village and ripping the place to shreds. . . .

The Special Forces became overpopulated with cowboys. You just had to look at the statistics as to how that organization grew and how the requirements for entrance changed. They suddenly dropped the cross-training and they suddenly dropped the requirement for languages. And pretty soon they started mass producing them because everybody wanted to wear a green beanie. And you get that caliber of person into a very hostile situation that requires a degree of sophistication — they didn't have it. It caused problems. And I think that's the demise of the Special Forces, to get some idiots out and shooting people in boats. I think it was because they had some concept of that's the way it was done. They watched too many John Wayne movies. It just wasn't that way.

— BRUCE LAWLOR, CENTRAL INTELLIGENCE AGENCY

. . .

The army of South Vietnam was being built up with American money and with the help of American advisors. At first these advisors were only trying to teach the Army of the Republic of Vietnam (ARVN) how to use the weapons the United States was supplying. Soon, however, uniformed American military personnel were joining ARVN troops in combat operations. American helicopters and their crewmen arrived. Although they were assigned simply to airlift South Vietnamese troops into battle, it wasn't long before their role had changed from providing mobility to providing power. Helicopters with mounted machine guns, rocket pods, and grenade launchers escorted unarmed helicopters into battle.

There was little publicity surrounding these changes in duties. Asked at a February 1962 news conference if U.S. troops were engaged in fighting in Vietnam, President Kennedy said they were not.

. . .

> ... the training missions we have [in South Vietnam] have been instructed that if they are fired upon, they are of course to fire back but we have not sent combat troops in [the] generally understood sense of the word.
>
> — PRESIDENT KENNEDY

. . .

Notes of caution voiced by some presidential advisors were discounted. Talk that someday hundreds of thousands of U.S. ground troops might be needed to keep Vietnam from communist rule was dismissed. The president called these predictions crazy.

Privately, however, Kennedy had misgivings.

·   ·   ·

They want a force of American troops. . . . They say it's necessary in order to restore confidence and maintain morale. But it will be just like Berlin. The troops will march in, the bands will play, the crowds will cheer, and in four days everyone will have forgotten. Then we will be told we have to send in more troops.

— PRESIDENT KENNEDY

·   ·   ·

But Kennedy continued on the course charted by Presidents Truman and Eisenhower. His decisions took America deeper into the quagmire that was to become the war.

The Buddhist Crisis

In May 1963 a crisis erupted that left no doubt that the Diem government was unstable. While Buddhism was the dominant religion in Vietnam, Diem's government was dominated by Catholics. Diem's repression of the Buddhists resulted in rioting in which nine people died, including women and children who were killed by his police.

·   ·   ·

Over three years, I watched Diem alienate one element of the society after another. . . . Then in the spring of '63 came the Buddhists. Even people in the embassy who knew nothing about politics were saying, ". . . He can't alienate the Buddhists." The ambassador was telling him "You've gotta settle with the Buddhists. . . ." But brother Nhu and Madame Nhu were saying ". . .We've got to smash the Buddhists."

— DOUGLAS PIKE, U.S. DEPARTMENT OF STATE

•   •   •

When the Buddhist demonstrations began against the Diem government, it became very clear to most Americans . . . that we were supporting a police state which, against its own people who were peaceably having demonstrations, would turn loose tanks and machine guns. . . .

— JAN BARRY, U.S. ARMY

•   •   •

On the morning of June 11, at a street corner near the Xa Loi Pagoda, an old sedan pulled up. A monk in saffron robe got out and squatted cross-legged on the pavement. Two other monks poured a can of gasoline over his head and robe while he fingered his prayer beads. Then the squatting monk calmly lit a match. Instantly he was enveloped in billowing flame and smoke. Except for involuntary muscular twitches, he sat impassively in the Buddhist attitude of prayer, palms

pressed together under his chin, until — after
three or four minutes — his charred body toppled
on its side in the street.

— JOHN MECKLIN, AMERICAN EMBASSY, SAIGON

•   •   •

In the United States the impact of the page one photograph of the martyred monk was profound. A significant
portion of the population was horrified by the act. Many
began to ask themselves if America should continue to
support the Diem government.

In early August 1963 there was a second suicide by a
Buddhist monk and three more (including a nun) over the
next two weeks.

•   •   •

... What have the Buddhist leaders done ...
the only thing they have done, they have barbe-
cued one of their monks.

If the Buddhists wish to have another barbecue
I will be glad to supply the gasoline and a match.

Let them burn and we shall clap our hands.

— MADAME NHU

•   •   •

Madame Nhu's callous comments did little to help the
already polarized political situation. Her husband offered to
furnish gasoline and matches to any American journalist
who wished to follow in the path of the monks.

•   •   •

The Buddhists bit, tasted a little political blood, bit harder, tasted more political blood, and then finally began to use American television . . . none of them spoke English but their signs were all in English.

And every time they planned a demonstration, or a Buddhist burned himself to death they would call up the American press. . . . So they learned to use the American . . . media for political purposes; they learned how to develop political power as they went along.

— ROGER HILSMAN, U.S. DEPARTMENT OF STATE

•　•　•

The Buddhists continued to protest and demonstrate; Diem continued to arrest, beat, and kill them.

The crisis spread throughout South Vietnam's cities, and the bitter resentment against the Diem regime now came to full flower. The militant monks offered other frustrated segments of the South Vietnamese population an outlet for their anti-Diem feelings.

The Buddhist crisis was a turning point in the relationship between Diem and the American government. The incredible suicides, coupled with Diem's violent repression, shattered any illusion that all was going well.

Diem's claim that the Buddhist protests were political and not religious paled before the fiery spectacle of people sacrificing their lives on the nightly news.

There were rumors that a coup d'état was being planned. The rumors were true.

Death of a President

If Diem's position in country continues deteriorate as result failure adopt proper political, psychological, economic and security measures, it may become necessary for US government to begin consideration alternative courses of action and leaders in order to achieve our objective.

— ELDRIDGE DURBROW, U.S. AMBASSADOR TO
SOUTH VIETNAM

•   •   •

We are prepared to continue to assist them (the South Vietnamese government), but I don't think the war can be won unless the people support the effort, and in my opinion, in the last two months the government has gotten out of touch with the people.

— PRESIDENT KENNEDY

•   •   •

I talked to, specifically to General Don, and I talked to other generals. And then this was the first indication that I had that there was really something serious going on — that there was actually a coup, so to speak, being thought of by senior officers of the Vietnamese army.

— LUCIEN CONEIN, CENTRAL INTELLIGENCE AGENCY

•   •   •

We wanted to be certain that if we succeeded with the coup we would have American support afterward, that the Americans agreed with us because we needed their aid to continue the war.

I asked Conein what the Americans thought. He said, yes, the Americans agree.

— GENERAL TRAN VAN DON, ARMY OF THE
REPUBLIC OF VIETNAM

• • •

During the whole reporting period, through my own channels, I was reporting every one of the developments leading up to and including the time of the coup. Every one of the . . . discussions that were held with . . . [the] military leaders who were participating in the coup was completely reported to Washington, D.C., and I received many times guidance of what I was to discuss. . . .

— LUCIEN CONEIN, CENTRAL INTELLIGENCE AGENCY

• • •

We are launched on a course from which there is no respectable turning back: the overthrow of the Diem government. There is no turning back in part because U.S. prestige is already publicly committed to this end. . . . In a more fundamental sense there is no turning back because there is no possibility, in my view, that the war can be won under a Diem administration. . . .

. . . it was just a little after one when we heard the first shell go off. And then we went up onto the roof and you could see the planes dropping bombs and you could see the troops starting to come down the street, and the thing was really on.

— HENRY CABOT LODGE, U.S. AMBASSADOR TO
SOUTH VIETNAM

• • •

On the afternoon of November 1, 1963, South Vietnamese troops under the leadership of the anti-Diem generals surrounded the presidential palace. Troops had also seized the city's radio stations, post office, airport, and police station.

Diem and his brother Nhu escaped that night — before the palace could be captured in the early hours of the morning. The next day they surrendered and, while being transported with their hands bound, were killed.

• • •

We had no alternative. They had to be killed.

— GENERAL DUONG VAN MINH,
HEAD OF THE MILITARY JUNTA

• • •

In the streets of Saigon the people rejoiced. The generals who were the new leaders of South Vietnam were offered bouquets of flowers and mobbed by the crowds. The U.S. ambassador was also cheered as a conquering hero. Within days, statues and posters of the ruling family had been destroyed.

Three weeks later, on November 22, 1963, President John F. Kennedy was assassinated in Dallas, Texas.

Vice-President Lyndon Baines Johnson assumed the presidency of the United States.

• • •

We are once again at the beginning of the beginning.
— MIKE MANSFIELD, SENATE MAJORITY LEADER

• • •

Part Two

Escalation

. . .

1964–1965

Chapter Four

the · t●nkin · gulf incident

FOR ALL I KNOW, OUR NAVY WAS SHOOTING
AT WHALES OUT THERE.

— PRESIDENT LYNDON BAINES JOHNSON

As VICE-PRESIDENT, LYNDON BAINES JOHNSON HAD SUP-
ported Kennedy's Vietnam policies.

. . .

. . . The battle against Communism must be
joined in Southeast Asia with strength and
determination to achieve success there . . .

We must decide whether to help these countries to the best of our ability or throw in the
towel in the area and pull back our defenses to . . .
a "Fortress America" concept. More important, we
would say to the world in this case that we don't
live up to our treaties and don't stand by our

friends. This is not my concept. I recommend that
we move forward promptly with a major effort to
help these countries defend themselves.

— VICE-PRESIDENT JOHNSON

• • •

Now, shortly after taking office, the new president re-
affirmed America's commitment to South Vietnam.

• • •

I am not going to lose Vietnam. I am not going
to be the President who saw Southeast Asia go the
way China went.

— PRESIDENT JOHNSON

• • •

The problems Johnson inherited, however, only got
worse. The coup, it appeared, had solved nothing. The ruling generals seemed reluctant to move against the Vietcong, the Vietnamese communist guerrilla forces in the
South. They were unenthusiastic about fighting the war
and were inept when it came to winning over their own
people. The generals who had taken over after Diem were
themselves ousted from power only three months after the
coup. The South Vietnamese government changed eight
times over the next two years.

• • •

After the Diem coup, General Big Minh, the
new leader of South Vietnam, was asking a lot of
political advice from the Americans in Saigon . . .
Big Minh asked Lodge, "What should I do polit-
ically?" And Lodge said, "Well, it's a little bit like

26

after Kennedy was assassinated. The American people were very upset and concerned about the future. So President Johnson went on television and explained that he was going to carry on. And this assured the American people. You need to re-assure the Vietnamese people."

Big Minh said, "Fine. Give us TV."

— RUFUS PHILLIPS, U.S. AGENCY FOR INTERNATIONAL DEVELOPMENT

. . .

In the course of my Ambassadorship which had been agreed to last just one year, I dealt with five governments, which meant five sets of senior generals, five sets of provincial chiefs governing forty-four provinces. In other words the house was cleaned — turned over — five different times with the chaos that one can imagine, and further-more from the outset there was no one firm gov-ernment at any time to build on.

— GENERAL MAXWELL TAYLOR, U.S. AMBASSADOR TO SOUTH VIETNAM

. . .

Actually no one on our side knew what the new people were thinking at all. It was a fantastic vacuum of information. Our requirements were really very simple — we wanted any government which would continue to fight.

— WILLIAM BUNDY, U.S. DEPARTMENT OF STATE

. . .

In a very real sense, South Vietnam is a country
with an army and no government.
— GEORGE BALL, U.S. DEPARTMENT OF STATE

• • •

By 1964 Ho Chi Minh had decided to increase the support the North Vietnamese were giving to the Vietcong.
Troops and supplies were sent down from North Vietnam
through a series of footpaths that ran north to south
through the jungles and mountains. These paths came to
be known as the Ho Chi Minh trail.

Vietcong terrorists began striking places where Americans congregated in Saigon and other areas of South Vietnam. Bombs killed and wounded Americans in bars, in
movie theaters, and on American bases.

Johnson's military advisors, as well as key members of
his administration, argued that the South Vietnamese government was unable to combat the communists. They
urged Johnson to increase the pressure on North Vietnam
by bombing Hanoi, the capital, and other targets.

A list of ninety-four targets in North Vietnam had been
developed in preparation for an air war.

To take the steps Johnson and his advisors were
contemplating, they needed congressional approval. Johnson had already prepared just such a request, but it had
been put aside. He was unsure of how Congress would
react to his request for an expanded war, and wanted to
be sure he picked the right moment — a moment when
not only Congress, but the country, would stand behind
him.

On August 4, 1964, in the waters of the Gulf of Tonkin

off the North Vietnamese coast, the right moment presented itself.

On August 2, 1964, the destroyer U.S.S. *Maddox* had been attacked by three North Vietnamese torpedo boats. The North Vietnamese probably associated the *Maddox* with recent attacks by South Vietnamese patrol boats.

The *Maddox* sank one of the North Vietnamese boats and crippled the other two. The *Maddox* had been hit by one bullet; there were no American casualties.

The next night the South Vietnamese again attacked North Vietnamese coastal installations.

What happened the next evening, August 4, is the subject of debate.

That night the *Maddox* intercepted a message interpreted as meaning that the North Vietnamese boats were going to attack again. The enemy craft appeared on the *Maddox*'s sonarscope shortly after and allegedly attacked. Crewmen saw the wakes of several torpedoes in the water. The sonar man confirmed the torpedo sightings, although U.S. Navy planes could not. The radar aboard the *Maddox* was, however, not functioning properly. The weather conditions were poor and the night was pitch black. The *Maddox* reported sinking two or three North Vietnamese torpedo boats and was not hit herself.

That evening the president informed the nation via a televised speech that American planes were in the process of retaliating for the attack.

. . .

Repeated acts of violence against the armed forces of the United States must be met not only with alert defense, but with positive reply. That reply is being given as I speak to you tonight.

— PRESIDENT JOHNSON

•   •   •

The next day the president sent to Congress the resolution that had been drafted earlier.

•   •   •

Resolved by the Senate and House of Representatives of the United States of America in Congress assembled, That the Congress approve and support the determination of the President, as Commander in Chief, to take all necessary measures to repel any armed attack against the forces of the United States and to prevent further aggression.

— THE TONKIN GULF RESOLUTION

•   •   •

Two days later Congress passed the Tonkin Gulf resolution by a vote of 416–0 in the House and 88–2 in the Senate.

Opinion polls showed that a majority of the American people also supported the president.

But Congress and the public had not been told all the facts associated with the incident.

Congress had not been informed that the *Maddox* had been involved in highly secret intelligence-gathering patrols in the Tonkin Gulf, patrols that also served as a show of force by the United States, and that had been taking place for months. During that time the United States had been involved in secret military attacks against the North Vietnamese, attacks that provoked the Tonkin Gulf incident, despite claims by the administration that the incident was unprovoked.

Johnson did not advise Congress or inform the public that he had, three months earlier, approved plans for air strikes against the North Vietnamese.

The Tonkin Gulf incident did not in fact take place — there was no North Vietnamese attack on the night of August 4. No one on the *Maddox* actually heard gunfire. Those who had seen something were not sure what they had seen. Disturbing atmospheric conditions might have affected the radar. The "torpedoes" might even have been the sounds of the *Maddox*'s own propellers.

·   ·   ·

> Entire action leaves many doubts. . . . Suggest thorough reconnaissance in daylight by aircraft. . . . Review of action makes many reported contacts and torpedoes fired appear very doubtful. . . . Freak weather effects and overeager sonarmen may have accounted for many reports. No actual sighting by Maddox. Suggest complete evaluation before any further action.
>
> — JOHN J. HERRICK, CHIEF OFFICER,
>   U.S.S. *MADDOX*

·   ·   ·

At that time, I felt it was questionable whether the second incident took place. I simply was not sure. It was not until after a number of days of collation of reports from the field had taken place that many of the reports which seemed to relate to the second incident were proved either to be unsound or to relate to the first incident.

That is what intelligence analysis is all about, and in a military situation, quite often the commanding officers — in this case, the President of the United States — don't wait for the details to be settled if they feel they are in a critical situation with a danger of military conflict. They make decisions without waiting for the intelligence detail.

— RAY CLINE, CENTRAL INTELLIGENCE AGENCY

• • •

The president had decided not to wait. In retaliation for the attack on the *Maddox*, sixty-four U.S. Navy bombers attacked torpedo boat bases and oil storage depots in North Vietnam. Two American planes were lost. The pilot of one had to parachute behind enemy lines.

• • •

I was among the first to launch off the carrier. Our squadron, ten airplanes, headed toward the target about four hundred miles away — a good two hours there and two hours back. It was sort of like a dream. We were actually going to war, into combat. I never thought it would happen, but all of a sudden here we were, and I was in it. I felt a little nervous. We made an identification pass, then came around and made an actual pass, firing. I was very low, just skimming the trees at about five hundred knots. Then I had the weirdest feeling. My airplane was hit and started to fall apart, rolling and burning. I knew I wouldn't live if I stayed with the airplane, so I ejected. . . .

— EVERETT ALVAREZ, JR. (POW 1964–1973)

. . .

The air war over North Vietnam had begun.

Chapter Five

rolling · thunder

BOMB 'EM BACK INTO THE STONE AGE.
— CURTIS LeMAY, U.S. AIR FORCE CHIEF OF STAFF

PRESIDENT LYNDON JOHNSON HOPED THAT BY EXHIBITING THE overwhelming superiority of American military technology he could convince the North Vietnamese that they could not win a war against the United States.

On March 2, 1965, Operation Rolling Thunder, the sustained aerial bombing of North Vietnam, began. It was to continue, with occasional halts, every day for three years.

• • •

I flew A-4 Skyhawks most of my career. It's a tactical aircraft, a bomber. . . . It's so small that you have to kind of slither in and get down into the seat. When they put the cockpit down, your shoulders are wedged against the sides, so when you fly the airplane, you feel like it's part of your body. . . .

I must confess I enjoyed the war part of it. It's phenomenal, the sense of euphoria to have come back from a mission where people were shooting at you. That's the ultimate gamble, your life versus theirs. Of course, you can't say it was real fair. . . . I was coming in with an A-4 with bombs and rockets and everything . . . there's no way to describe the euphoria. If you took the guys coming into the locker room after the Super Bowl, even though they're getting a lot more money and they're greater heroes in front of 75,000 cheering people, that's probably 50 percent of what post-strike euphoria is like if they really shoot at you.

. . . You're flying these missions two or three times a day. . . . You're sitting there in your flight suit. The plane is loaded. The bombs are on it. . . . All of a sudden the bell rings. You leap up. You run and jump in the airplane. You buckle yourself in. . . . The guy comes running up behind you with your knee board with the coordinates. While you're strapping in and putting your helmet on, the guy's starting the engine up. You give him the signal and start the plane. You roll out of the chocks and you're gone. *Zzzhhhoooooom.*

— JOHN BUCHANAN, U.S. MARINES

•   •   •

When I first spotted Vietnam — when I first spotted the country from the plane — is when I really started to understand that there's really a war going on here. . . . I could tell by looking at the countryside. There were bomb craters . . . everywhere. I mean, it wasn't as if you saw a nice beautiful forest and then you went in and saw a battleground then. The whole country was covered with craters.

— CHARLES SABATIER, U.S. ARMY

. . .

My first impression when we crossed the DMZ was that somebody had turned the goddamn place into the moon. I've never seen so many bomb craters in my whole life. I was appalled. And the thing that really got me was the city of Dong Hoi. It was the first major city north of the DMZ. . . . they had bombed that thing right into the Stone Age. All you could see was foundations. There was not a stick standing. Totally destroyed. Absolutely, completely destroyed. There wasn't a living soul there. . . .

— DICK RUTAN, U.S. AIR FORCE

. . .

The bombing started at about eight o'clock in the morning and lasted for hours. At the first sound of explosions, we rushed into the tunnels, but not everyone made it. During a pause in the attack, some of us climbed out to see what we could do, and the scene was terrifying. Bodies had been torn to pieces — limbs hanging from trees or scattered around the ground. Then the bombing began again, this time with napalm, and the village went up in flames. The napalm hit me, and I must have gone crazy. I felt as if I were burning all over, like charcoal, and I lost consciousness. Comrades took me to the hospital, and my wounds didn't begin to heal until six months later. More than two hundred people died in the raid, including my mother, my sister-in-law and three nephews. They were buried alive when their tunnel collapsed.

— HO THANH DAM, NORTH VIETNAMESE CIVILIAN

. . .

There were 25,000 sorties the first year of Rolling Thunder, 79,000 the next, and over 100,000 in 1967. Roads, vehicles, railway lines, fuel and storage depots were hit again and again.

Johnson closely monitored the bombing as American bombers destroyed nearly all military and industrial targets in North Vietnam. The financial cost of the air war was staggering: The United States was spending ten dollars for every dollar's worth of damage done to the enemy.

But despite the awesome power and the impressive statistics the air war was failing.

. . .

. . . the problem in the North was that the targets were elusive. . . . during the night, all the trucks and storage areas would move. That was coupled with the fact that the pilots had never been there before, and they were going up in this hostile area to try to find this target and bomb it. The success rate was terrible.

— DICK RUTAN, U.S. AIR FORCE

• • •

I was convinced that we were not going to achieve our will by bombing the North; that in the first place, it was a fairly primitive industrial society, and that there weren't the kind of targets that were adapted for strategic bombing. And secondly, I was convinced that we would never break the will of a determined people simply by bombing; and in fact, we would probably tend to unite them more than ever.

— GEORGE BALL, U.S. DEPARTMENT OF STATE

• • •

. . . Everybody thought, Oh, boy, we're sending American airplanes up and they'll bomb a couple of targets and the other side will be terrified. . . . I personally thought it would be a token of U.S. resolve, and a sample of what we could do. I really thought it would impress them. I now think it just infuriated them. And we just kept doing it. We did more and more and more . . . and it was never enough. We never quite grasped the fact that the North Vietnamese intended to win. Regardless.

— GENERAL WILLIAM DE PUY

• • •

The aerial bombing was neither intimidating the North Vietnamese leadership nor weakening the will of the people.

. . .

There was extraordinary fervor then. The Americans thought that the more bombs they dropped, the quicker we would fall to our knees and surrender. But the bombs heightened rather than dampened our spirit.

— Ton That Tung, North Vietnamese civilian

. . .

It must not be forgotten that General Curtis Lemay had said that the United States should bomb Vietnam back into the Stone Age. But they were greatly mistaken. The destruction of the North — with all the efforts and all the barbarity of imperial America — only caused the people to be more resilient and more resolute in their determination to resist and to win.

— Pham Von Dong, Prime Minister,
North Vietnam

. . .

Painstaking procedures were implemented by the North Vietnamese to protect the civilian population. There were mass evacuations from the cities to the countryside. In Hanoi shelters big enough for one person were built every few feet. Trenches were dug along roads so people could take cover quickly. Tunnels were constructed by peasants from their villages to their fields. This allowed them to continue to work while giving them a place to hide when the planes appeared overhead. After a raid civilian teams rescued people caught beneath the rubble and administered first aid and got them to the hospital.

Thousands worked repairing roads, railroads, and bridges soon after they were hit.

The communists developed a formidable air defense capability that included a complex, computerized Soviet radar system. U.S. planes, shot down while attempting to hit their targets, resulted in the first American prisoners of war.

And Operation Rolling Thunder was killing Vietnamese civilians in greater numbers than the United States was willing to admit. American claims of "surgical" air strikes that only hit military targets were shown to be false.

One of Rolling Thunder's main targets was the Ho Chi Minh trail. Johnson wanted to stop the North Vietnamese from sending troops and supplies down this primitive system of jungle paths into South Vietnam. If that supply route could be cut, the war in the South could be severely affected.

Rolling Thunder was unable to stop or even impede the flow of soldiers and arms South. In fact, the North Vietnamese were coming into the South in increased numbers: 35,000 in 1965 and 90,000 by 1967. The communists stepped up the intensity of their attacks in the South. The bombing campaign was doing little to help the ARVN troops, who continued to be defeated by the Vietcong.

Throughout the war the Pentagon recommended intensifying the bombing. But Secretary of Defense McNamara, long one of the main architects of the war, could see that Rolling Thunder was not the answer.

•   •   •

No amount of bombing can end the war.

... enemy operations in the south cannot, on the basis of any reports I have seen, be stopped by air bombardment — short, that is, of the virtual annihilation of North Vietnam and its people.

— ROBERT MCNAMARA, SECRETARY OF DEFENSE

•　•　•

... the idea that destroying, or threatening to destroy, North Vietnam's industry would pressure Hanoi into calling it quits seems, in retrospect, a colossal misjudgment.

— DEFENSE INTELLIGENCE AGENCY ANALYSIS

•　•　•

Let's get one thing clear. I am not going to stop the bombing. I have heard every argument on the subject, and I am not interested in further discussion. I have made up my mind. I'm not going to stop it.

— PRESIDENT JOHNSON

•　•　•

Part Three

Americanization
. . .

1965–1967

Chapter Six

in·country

If the war is to be won, then it must be done by the Vietnamese — nothing would be more foolhardy than the employment of U.S. . . . troops in quantity. We could pour our entire Army into Vietnam — and accomplish nothing worthwhile.

— John Paul Vann, U.S. Army

· · ·

You know . . . there are people at State and the Pentagon who want to send *three hundred thousand* men out there. But the President will never get sucked into anything like that.

— Vice-President Hubert H. Humphrey

· · ·

. . . we saw that the U.S. support base was growing like a goddamned mushroom. Every time we'd take a trip back to Nha Trang, Da Nang or Cam Ranh Bay we could see this tremendous buildup coming. More and more permanent-type installations were being built. . . . I figured, "Something is going to happen. We're going to be here a long time."

— Chuck Allen,
U.S. Army Special Forces

Ground Troops

IN EARLY 1965 GENERAL WILLIAM WESTMORELAND, WHO became commander of U.S. military forces in Vietnam in June 1964, requested that two U.S. Marine Corps battalions be sent to South Vietnam.

· · ·

When the bombing program started, I realized that the airfields — we had three jet-capable airfields — were extremely vulnerable. If that strategy was to be a viable one, we had to protect those airfields. I feared that the Vietnamese did not have the capability of protecting the American aircraft on those airfields, and therefore, my first request for troops was associated with protecting the airfields.

— GENERAL WILLIAM WESTMORELAND,
COMMANDER, MILITARY ASSISTANCE
COMMAND, VIETNAM

· · ·

The air war, implemented in part to avoid a bloody ground war, was now, itself, the reason for the presence of ground troops.

On March 8, 1965, U.S. Marines carrying M-16's and dressed in full battle gear waded ashore at Red Beach Two, north of Danang. They were greeted by sightseers, ARVN officers, and Vietnamese girls who looped garlands of flowers around their necks. The White House issued a statement that explained that the Marines were only there to protect American facilities. They would not engage the

Vietcong other than to ensure the security of those air-fields.

By granting Westmoreland's request Lyndon Johnson had become the first American president to authorize ground troops for offensive operation in South Vietnam.

At first the Marines were limited to patrolling no further than eighty-five kilometers from the base. But in less than a month that changed.

.   .   .

The first troops were invited in to protect our air bases. Now once those troops were at those bases, it made no sense at all to have them dig in and go strictly on the defensive.

— GENERAL WESTMORELAND

.   .   .

... our objective ... to defend that big complex at Danang ... You can't defend a place like that by sitting on your ditty-box. You've got to get out and aggressively patrol. And that's what people are doing. And the one thing I emphasized to them while I was out there was to find these Viet-cong and kill them.

— GENERAL WALLACE GREENE, JR.,
COMMANDANT, U.S. MARINE CORPS

.   .   .

In July 1965 Westmoreland requested an immediate troop increase to 125,000 men and another 75,000 by the end of the year. Johnson agreed and also increased the monthly draft quotas to 35,000.

The 500,000 young men and women arriving "in country" during 1965–1967 came from all parts of the United States and for a variety of reasons. They found a different country and a different war than in previous years.

. . .

It was 1964 when I signed up and 1965 when I graduated. At that time, there wasn't really much news about Vietnam. I didn't know what was going on there. I had no idea that Vietnam was going to be a major part of my life.

— MARY STOUT, U.S. ARMY NURSE

. . .

The soldiers got a great deal of support from the States. Classes by the hundreds would write letters addressed to a soldier in Vietnam, and these were packed up and sent to our unit, and by and large, the soldiers would try to respond to these things. There was a groundswell of popular support behind the troops in 1965.

— TED DANIELSEN

. . .

21 May 66

Dear Class C-4,

South Vietnam is a very small country struggling to keep its freedom. Many of the little boys and girls in South Vietnam may never have the opportunities that you children will have. Nevertheless, the children of South Vietnam are very much like yourselves in the games they play and the things they do. I am enclosing some paper toys that the boys and girls of Vietnam play with. I hope that you enjoy the toys as much as they do. In Vietnam, the little things mean a lot more than the big things.

It is nice to know that you children are safe and sound in America. The reason that I and all the other soldiers are in Vietnam is so that you children will always be safe in our great country. Thank you all again for thinking of me in this strange land. I hope that all the soldiers in Vietnam have as many boys and girls thinking about [them] as I do.

Sincerely yours,
PFC Robert B. Jackman
— ROBERT B. JACKMAN, U.S. ARMY

. . .

I had been accepted . . . at several colleges . . . by my senior year. And then I just decided, no, I'm gonna join the Marines. And I had to spend a lot of time talking to my parents about it, because at 17, of course, I would not have been allowed to sign an enlistment contract in my own right. They had to sign it too, and really what I think tipped the scales in the discussion was at one point, after talking for a long time, I said, "Mom, is this the way you raised me, to let other mothers' sons fight America's wars?" And they were young people during World War II. They believed in their country and that was it. They hadn't raised me that way.

. . . when the government said that the Communists were taking over Vietnam, and if we didn't stop them there we would have to stop them eventually in San Diego, I took that at face value. And I saw my opportunity to really be a hero.

— WILLIAM EHRHART, U.S. MARINES

. . .

When I quit high school, I went down to the army recruiter and just walked in and said, "I want to join the army." He said, "Sure, fine. Just take the tests, and we'll talk to you." I took all the tests, and he called me into his office and said, "Look, you scored the highest in the automotive section of the test." I said, "I expected to score the lowest there. I never even saw the inside of a car. I guessed at everything on that." He said, "All right. The second highest score was clerical." I said, "I don't want clerical." He ran down the field, and I kept saying, "No, I don't like that," so he said, "Well, what do you want?" "I want to become an infantryman, and I want to go to Vietnam." "You want to go to Vietnam?" "Yeah." He said, "You got it. . . ."

— DONALD HINES, U.S. ARMY

. . .

December 5, 1966

Dear Folks,

Arrived at Oakland, California, in good shape. Took regular Army bus to base. Mom: the chow we ate, gulped, is oily, tasteless and mean to me stomach. Went through some processing till Friday and then abruptly left for the trip over.

Stopped at Anchorage, Alaska, for a cool hour, and then a long hop to Tokyo before landing at Saigon's airport: Tan Son Nhut.

The first thing you notice going down the ramp is a heavy, lousy, sweet smell that floods your nose, along with a somewhat dirty feeling all around. Inside the makeshift customs building, the heat you didn't notice before begins to flush your head as sweat starts to flow. Answer a few questions, surrender any guns, knives and drugs, and be quiet, we are told. . . .

We then left by bus for Long Binh, 22 miles northeast of Saigon, for more processing. A cruddy place, typical of an Army camp put up in a hurry. Passed through sections of a town that are something like our Coney Island, "honky tonk" with dirt everywhere. Sanitation seems non-existent. Hope better awaits.

Regards,

Rick

— RICHARD LOFFLER, U.S. ARMY

• • •

. . . They couldn't fly us into Long Binh because it was too late at night, so we landed in Danang and stayed in the nurses' barracks. The next day they flew us to Bien Hoa and bused us in to Long Binh. I tell you, when I got there, I just sat and looked and said to myself, "What am I doing here? Here I came all these thousands of miles — why am I here?"

. . . the whole country . . . smelled bad. . . . I think for the whole thirteen months I couldn't get used to the smell of it. When I first got there, it was just like you'd gag because it smelled horrible.

— PINKIE HOUSER, U.S. ARMY

· · ·

Anyway, we land in Tan Son Nhut. It's about ten o'clock, and it's dark. When the plane comes down, it just drops — it's not like a long, gradual descent. You're just down. The reason, they told us, was to keep from getting shot down. I remember saying to the major, "Well, that's interesting."

— ANN POWLAS, U.S. ARMY NURSE

· · ·

. . . I went over on the aircraft carrier, the USS *Boxer*. After a very violent cruise we pulled up to the coast of Vietnam. Over the PA system they said, *"We are now off the coast of Vietnam. You can go up on the flight deck and take a look."* We all had this feeling that we were going to see a war going on — artillery exploding, jets strafing. I remember getting up on the flight deck and seeing one of the most beautiful visions I've ever seen in my life . . . a beautiful white beach with thick jungle background. . . . I said, "Wait a minute, wait a minute, what's going on here? We must have the wrong place."

We came down off the *Boxer* on wet nets into these landing crafts. Everybody saw the movies going on in their heads, thinking we would be getting shot at. It was the movies, except it was real. . . .

They opened the front of the craft. We started to charge in the water. All of a sudden I thought, "What the hell is going on here?" It was General Westmoreland and his whole brigade of generals. They were all lined up on the beach ... saluting the Cav on the way into Vietnam. The only thing missing was the hula girls with the leis. What a letdown.

— THOMAS BIRD, U.S. ARMY

.   .   .

Cherries

... you watch the cherries come in, the replacements. Instead of carrying a combat pack, they have huge rucksacks. They're carrying shaving cream, aftershave, razors. They have undershirts, underwear, notebooks, pens, a ton of stupid stuff. You see them on patrol trying to climb a hill, and they're sliding backward. Then you grab them and say, "Look. You can throw out the undershirts. You won't need them here. The underpants, too. And the clean socks. You don't take your boot off in combat." A few crazies did take them off at night, but I never took mine off until given new ones. If there's an attack, how are you going to operate without boots in the jungle full of spines and pungi sticks?

— ANGEL QUINTANA, U.S. ARMY

.   .   .

I remember one night patrol. We were walking over an area of sand dunes. A VC armed with a weapon ran across the trail in front of our point man. He was a new guy, his first night patrol. The VC stopped, looked at him and kept on running. The point man could have very easily shot him, but what he said was "Halt, who goes there?" I remember the squad leader saying, "Did you really . . . say that? Did you really . . . say, 'Halt, who goes there'?"

— DOUGLAS ANDERSON, U.S. MARINES

• • •

The first time you were under fire, you thought, "How . . . can they do this to me? If only I could talk to the . . . firing at me, we'd get along, everything would be all right." I just had the overwhelming feeling that if I could talk to these people, that they really are the same as I am, that it's not us that are doing it, it's some other system and we're just pawns in this . . . thing, throwing the shit at each other.

— LEE CHILDRESS, U.S. ARMY

• • •

As soon as the plane landed we . . . got onto these buses. A typical bus, except that it looked like prison buses, army green prison buses with wire mesh over the windows. And I asked why . . . this kind of bus. I thought we were in friendly country. . . . And they told me it was to stop the people from running and throwing grenades into the bus. Oh my God, you mean people are trying to kill me? Wait a minute. . . . I never really thought about dying before.

— CHARLES SABATIER, U.S. ARMY

.   .   .

. . . you would go through the villages, and you learned right away that you weren't loved in Vietnam. Okay? Right from the start. I think that was the crazy part. We would go through villages, riding on the truck . . . and these little kids would stand there and stick their . . . finger up at you. These were little kids. I couldn't believe it. . . . They were always sticking their finger out or begging for food . . . and I hated them.

— LEONARD C. WILSON, U.S. ARMY

.   .   .

I'd say the light turned on for me when I went through that little mud-encrusted village with grass huts . . . and . . . Saw the people, saw the looks on their faces. . . . A certain fear and hostility. I suppose it's the look of someone who sees an enemy but doesn't want to provoke him. Withdrawn. Clearly people on the other side.

— JOHN CUSHMAN, U.S. ARMY

.   .   .

I remember most how hard it was to just shoot people.

I remember one time when three of our people got killed by sniper fire from this village. We went over to burn the village down. I was afraid that there was going to be shootin' people that day, so I just kind of dealt with the animals. You know, shoot the chickens. I mean I just couldn't shoot no people.

I don't know how many chickens I shot. But it was a little pig that freaked me out more than the chickens. You think you gonna be shootin' a little pig, it's just gonna fall over and die. Well, no. His little guts be hangin' out. He just be squiggling around and freakin' you out.

See, you got to shoot animals in the head. If we shoot you in your stomach, you may just fall over and die. But an animal, you got to shoot them in the head. They don't understand that they supposed to fall over and die.

— REGINALD "MALIK" EDWARDS, U.S. MARINES

•   •   •

A couple of us were just kind of hanging loose out in front of the main hospital building, which was a big corrugated-tin prefab. About forty new guys were lined up there to have their shot records checked before being sent to their units.

The guys were all new, their first couple of days in-country, and they were all wondering what it was going to be like. Joking, smoking cigarettes, playing grab-ass in the line — it was pretty loose. I mean, nobody was saying, "Straighten up. Stand in formation," none of that. People were just kind of leaning up against the building.

All of a sudden four choppers came in and they

didn't even touch down. They just dumped bags. One of the bags broke open and what came out was hardly recognizable as a human being. For those of us that were just sort of standing there looking in the direction of the new guys . . . it's not the kind of thing you laugh at. . . . All the guys stopped laughing. Nobody was saying anything. And some people were shaking and some people were throwing up, and one guy got down and started to pray.

I said to myself, "Welcome to the war, boys."

— DAVID ROSS, U.S. ARMY

•　•　•

Chapter Seven
winning · hearts
and · minds

THIS ISN'T A WAR FOR TERRITORY, IT'S A WAR FOR THE
HEARTS AND THE MINDS OF THE PEOPLE.

— JOHN K. WALKER, U.S. ARMY

MANY AMERICANS MADE EFFORTS TO WIN OVER THE SOUTH
Vietnamese people. They provided medical aid, agricultural expertise, engineering know-how, and other assistance. It was hoped that these efforts would help show the peasants the benefits of democracy. And that this would help win their allegiance in the fight against the communists.

• • •

We were well indoctrinated with the Nine-Rule
Card, which I still carry: . . . we are guests in this
country and we are here to help these people. We
had a strong indoctrination in "help." . . . incredibly idealistic. We never had much indoctrination
about the Vietnamese according to their culture,

their traditions, how different they were going to be. They were shockingly different from the moment we got there. We had never experienced a people like that in our lives. We all had a tremendous big-brother ego, everybody gave the kids something to eat.

— THOMAS BIRD, U.S. ARMY

. . .

They were the most patient people. . . . You'd get there about eight in the morning and there would be half a dozen people sitting there with their babies, or injured children, or sitting beside somebody on a stretcher, just waiting for somebody to come. . . . I remember one cute little bright-eyed . . . kid . . . who'd been shot through the lung. I operated on him and the dressings were painful. I had nothing for the pain, so I would talk to him. Mostly body language . . . I knew I'd hurt him, I could see the tears in his eyes, but he would not call out. When I finished the dressing, I didn't happen to have a stethoscope, so I put my head down to listen to his chest to see if his lungs were expanding or anything. And this kid grabbed me around the neck and gave me a big hug and the biggest smile I've ever seen. This after I'd just hurt him.

— BEALE ROGERS, VOLUNTEER DOCTOR

. . .

The thing I remember most about Vietnam was the kids. I think almost everybody liked the kids. I

never saw kids that smiled so much. It didn't matter if they were up to their chins in shit, they just
kept on smiling. We did a lot of work in schools.
We'd go into schools and teach them how to
brush their teeth. We'd go out to the camps and
the kids would always come around. Or we'd go
out into a village and find a wild pineapple and
start slicing it up. All of a sudden you had five or
six kids sitting on your knees, all eating the
pineapple . . .

— DAVID ROSS, U.S. ARMY

•   •   •

But these efforts were doomed to failure for a variety of
reasons. For one thing the Americans, although at times
genuine in their efforts to help, were becoming more and
more confusing and cruel. The South Vietnamese, who at
first viewed the Americans as strange, exotic creatures,
had learned to fear them.

•   •   •

Artillery from our ships will soon hit your village. You must look for cover immediately. From
now on, chase the Vietcong away from your village, so the government won't have to shell your
area again.

— LEAFLET NO. APO-6227, U.S. ARMY'S
PSYCHOLOGICAL WARFARE OFFICE

•   •   •

We would go through a village before dawn,
rousting everybody out of bed, and kicking down
doors and dragging them out if they didn't move

fast enough. They all had underground bunkers inside their huts to protect themselves against bombing and shelling. But to us the bunkers were Vietcong hiding places, and we'd blow them up with dynamite — and blow up the huts too. If we spotted extra rice lying around, we'd confiscate it to keep them from giving it to the Vietcong. . . . At the end of the day, the villagers would be turned loose. Their homes had been wrecked, their chickens killed, their rice confiscated — and if they weren't pro-Vietcong before we got there, they sure as hell were by the time we left.

— WILLIAM EHRHART, U.S. MARINES

. . .

The day's operation burned down 150 houses, wounded three women, killed one baby, wounded one marine and netted these four prisoners. Four old men who could not answer questions put to them in English. Four old men who had no idea what an I.D. card was. Today's operation is the frustration of Vietnam in miniature. There is little doubt that American firepower can win a military victory here. But to a Vietnamese peasant whose home . . . means a lifetime of backbreaking labor — it will take more than presidential promises to convince him that we are on his side.

— MORLEY SAFER, CBS NEWS

. . .

In 1965, I made a return visit to Vietnam. I went to see a friend named Chau. . . . We got to talking about what was going on. He said, "I just can't make any sense out of what the hell the Americans are doing. Do they have some plan?" I looked at him, I got tears in my eyes, and said, "Chau, I wish I could tell you that the Americans have a plan. But I have to be honest with you. They don't have a plan. We really don't know what the hell we're doing."

— Rufus Phillips, U.S. Agency for
International Development

. . .

It was a hot afternoon and I was tending our water buffalo in the fields, prodding it left and right with a bamboo stick and daydreaming when the motor noise began. . . .

But this motor noise was different. Like a tiger growling in a cave, the hollow noise became a roar and our buffalo grunted and trotted without prodding toward the trees. Steadily, the roar increased and I looked into the sun to see two helicopters, whining and flapping like furious birds, settle out of the sky toward me. The wind whipped my clothes and snatched the sun hat from my head. Even the ankle-deep water itself retreated before the down blast of their terrible beating winds. What could a puny girl do but fall down on her knees and hold fast to mother earth?

To my surprise, I did not die. Almost as quickly as it arrived, the roar spun down and the dying blast of wind and water gave back the heat of the day. As I raised my eyes, the dull green door on the side of the ship slid open and the most splendid man I had ever seen stepped onto the marshy ground.

He was a giant ... crispy clean in starched fatigues with a yellow scarf tucked into his shirt and a golden patch upon his shoulder. The black boots into which his battle pants were bloused shone bright as a beetle's shell.

Still cowering, I watched his brawny, blond-haired hands raise binoculars to his eyes. He scanned the tree line around Ky La, ignoring me completely, and chewed the lip below his scruffy mustache. In a husky voice, he said something in his queer language to another fair-skinned soldier inside the door, then dropped the field glasses to his chest and climbed back inside his machine.

Instantly the flap-flap-flap and siren howl increased and the typhoon rose again. As if plucked by the hand of god, the enormous green machine tiptoed on its skids and swooped away, climbing steadily toward the treetops, the second craft behind it. In seconds even the hollow growl was gone. . . .

. . . it was awe, not courage, that nailed my feet to the ground when the Americans landed. In time, we all would learn the wisdom of standing still at the approach of Americans — the way one learns to stand still in the face of an angry dog. Before long, any Vietnamese who ran from American gunships would be considered Viet Cong and shot down for the crime of fear.

— LE LY HAYSLIP, SOUTH VIETNAMESE CIVILIAN

.   .   .

Chapter Eight

arvn

THIS IMPORTANT WAR MUST BE FOUGHT AND WON BY THE
VIETNAMESE THEMSELVES. WE HAVE KNOWN THIS FROM THE
BEGINNING. BUT THE DISCOURAGING TRUTH IS THAT . . . WE
HAVE NOT FOUND THE FORMULA . . . FOR TRAINING AND
INSPIRING THEM INTO EFFECTIVE ACTION.

— ROBERT MCNAMARA, SECRETARY OF DEFENSE

. . .

A MISERABLE . . . PERFORMANCE, JUST LIKE IT ALWAYS IS.

— JOHN PAUL VANN, U.S. ARMY

PERHAPS THE MOST IMPORTANT REASON THE EFFORT TO WIN
over the South Vietnamese was failing was the lack of
support from the South Vietnamese government and its
army — the Army of the Republic of Vietnam (ARVN).
Both continued to be a burden, rather than a help.

. . .

The thing that worried Johnson — and con-
stantly worried him — was the instability of the
South Vietnamese government . . . the coat of
arms of the Vietnamese government was a turn-
style, for God's sake. And, . . . I remember very

vividly somebody would come in his office and say, "Looks like there's a coup beginning in Vietnam." There'd be another coup. You know, coups were like fleas on a dog, and Johnson said, "I don't want to hear any more about this coup shit. I've had enough of it, and we've got to find a way to stabilize those people out there."

— JACK VALENTI, PRESIDENTIAL AIDE

·   ·   ·

Johnson urged the government to offer the South Vietnamese people democratic processes, like free elections and economic changes that would help alleviate poverty and disease.

The South Vietnamese rulers refused. They resented what they considered American intrusion into their affairs. They wanted, as with governments in the past, American money and American military might, but not American advice.

The army was worse.

In January 1963, ARVN officers had, in a key battle, refused to help rescue downed American helicopter crewmen, or even to come to the aid of their fellow Vietnamese soldiers. They had disregarded orders from the top-ranking American advisors and even refused to obey commands from their direct South Vietnamese superiors. In the heat of battle, ARVN commanders who had previously understood English acted as if they didn't.

ARVN "armchair" generals seemed to prefer commanding from the relative safety of Saigon, rather than out in the countryside where the enemy was. Officers, with few exceptions, were more interested in filling their pocket-books than winning the war. There were reports that some sold much-needed gasoline and medicine to their own troops for personal profit. Others were known to charge their countrymen for artillery support during battle.

ARVN units sometimes took hours to reach battle sites only a mile or two from their own positions. And when they did arrive, they were often ineffective, cowardly, or both. They maneuvered their American-supplied armored personnel carriers (APCs) behind downed helicopters in order to hide. Machine gunners fired blindly, too frightened to expose themselves in order to see where they were shooting. ARVN infantry in the rice paddies held their rifles over their heads and they too shot blindly in order to avoid injury or death. South Vietnamese soldiers sometimes fired on their own troops in confusion and panic.

. . .

Young American Army officers who came to Vietnam as advisors were . . . not prepared for a system where incompetents were given commands for political reasons, where a battle was lost because a company commander was a coward and was not then relieved. . . .

There were . . . numerous instances when their [ARVN] officers found ways not to give the order to attack. [They] undeniably lacked . . . "motivation," that elusive spark in the human spirit that makes a man go the extra, seemingly suicidal ten yards that it takes to overrun an enemy position. As our field advisors put it, the government

forces, officers and men alike, were convinced that the Viet Cong were "eight feet tall."
— JOHN MECKLIN, AMERICAN EMBASSY, SAIGON

. . .

American soldiers believed that the ARVN purposely avoided contact with the enemy — refusing to attack where they were. At times ARVN soldiers deliberately made noise to warn the Vietcong to avoid confronting them in battle. Some ARVN soldiers were reported running from the field of battle because they were frightened at what turned out to be the sound of their own planes.

The ARVN alienated the peasants by stealing their food and abusing their families.

It was estimated that one out of every three South Vietnamese soldiers drafted, deserted within the first two months. In 1965 twice as many deserted as the year before.

. . .

One of the first things that I began to wonder about — really wonder about — is the soldiers who were our allies, the Army of the Republic. We called them ARVN — they wouldn't fight! At least in our area, in heavily populated civilian areas where the enemy was literally the old farmer by day, fighter by night kind of thing. With virtually no equipment except what they could capture from the American and the ARVN, tremendously outnumbered, the Vietcong were there day after day picking away at us. . . . And it occurred to me that these are the same people. The ARVN and the VC are the same people, the same race, the same culture, and yet one side seems to be chicken and the other side seems to fight in the face of overwhelming disadvantages. And I started wondering why . . . is this?

— WILLIAM EHRHART, U.S. MARINES

. . .

Sometimes they'd have an accidental weapon discharge while on patrol in the woods. That was nothing more than a signal to let the VC know we were coming. Because they didn't want to get into a firefight. Or at night we'd catch them cooking rice with an eight-foot bonfire smoking up the whole valley, letting everybody know where we were.

We knew damn well that they wanted to give away their positions to try and avoid a firefight. . . .

— CHUCK ALLEN, U.S. ARMY SPECIAL FORCES

. . .

. . . They shot artillery like it was going out of style . . . I once found a Vietnamese unit firing artillery ammunition so they could get the boxes it came in to make furniture. These 105mm rounds were shipped all the way from the U.S. in boxes. There were two rounds to a box . . . These were quite good boxes, very useful for building walls, beds or desks. . . .

— JOHN H. CUSHMAN, U.S. ARMY

. . .

Chapter Nine

guerrilla·war

GUERRILLA WARFARE IS THE MEANS WHEREBY THE PEOPLE
OF A WEAK, BADLY EQUIPPED COUNTRY CAN STAND UP
AGAINST AN AGGRESSIVE ARMY POSSESSING BETTER
EQUIPMENT AND TECHNIQUES.

— VO NGUYEN GIAP, COMMANDER IN CHIEF,

NORTH VIETNAMESE ARMY

. . .

WHEN ENGAGING A STRONGER ENEMY: . . . WITHDRAW WHEN
HE ADVANCES; HARASS HIM WHEN HE STOPS; STRIKE HIM
WHEN HE IS WEARY; PURSUE HIM WHEN HE WITHDRAWS. . . .
THE ENEMY MUST BE HARASSED, ATTACKED, DISPERSED,
EXHAUSTED AND ANNIHILATED.

GUERRILLAS ARE LIKE FISH, AND THE PEOPLE ARE THE WATER
IN WHICH THE FISH SWIM.

— MAO ZEDONG, CHAIRMAN OF THE PEOPLE'S

REPUBLIC OF CHINA

THE VIETCONG GUERRILLAS AVOIDED DIRECT ENGAGEMENTS
with American troops unless conditions were over-

whelmingly in their favor. Lacking air power and artillery support, they substituted mobility, ingenuity, dedication, and knowledge of the terrain. The Vietcong used the jungles, the mountains, the swamps, and the rain forests to their benefit. They built elaborate underground tunnel complexes and put together crudely made but efficient mines of wood or even cardboard. Although their weapons were of poor quality, they made the most of what they had.

. . .

They could booby-trap *everything*. A cigarette package — anything — and leave it around. There was unbelievable terror of everything booby-trapped. . . .

— TOM HAGEL, U.S. ARMY

. . .

We faced mostly local VC, peasants armed with World War II rifles and no heavy weapons. They were taking on the best army in the world. . . . We respected them from day one . . . they always hit us where we were the weakest. They always decided when, where, and how to fight us; on what terrain and under what conditions; and when to break away and melt into the local populace or go back down into their tunnels. They decided when to conduct ambushes or raids, plant booby traps, employ snipers. . . . They did an awful lot with an awful little. . . .

They were tremendously inventive. We used to capture homemade rifles created out of metal pipes and bits of fence post. We never put out antipersonnel mines: We knew they would be dug up and used against us. Claymores were strictly accounted for, but they still were stolen. We always worried about Charlie getting sophisticated weapons. Once our whole battalion was roused out at night and sent looking for a starlight scope which was lost. We found it. We really worried about him getting a field piece. . . . The Vietnamese were just so ingenious. We all knew they were poor, not stupid.

— THOMAS GILTNER, U.S. ARMY

. . .

For American soldiers, simply identifying the enemy, in a war where there were no front lines, had become a nightmare.

. . .

. . . In this type of fighting it was almost impossible to know who the enemy was at any one time. Children were suspect, women were suspect.

— DOUGLAS ANDERSON, U.S. MARINES

. . .

The guy who might have been your cook during the day, or the guy across the street cutting hair . . . that night he'd put on his black pajamas and bring his AK-47 out from under his mattress. He went out to your camp and was shooting at you.

— DAN PITZER, U.S. ARMY SPECIAL FORCES

. . .

. . . They all looked alike. They all dressed alike. They were all Vietnamese. Some of them were Vietcong. Here's a woman of twenty-two or twenty-three. She is pregnant, and she tells an interrogator that her husband works in Danang and isn't a Vietcong. But she watches your men walk down a trail and get killed or wounded by a booby trap. She knows the booby trap is there, but she doesn't warn them. Maybe she planted it herself. It wasn't like the San Francisco Forty-Niners on one side of the field and the Cincinnati Bengals on the other. The enemy was all around you.

— E. J. BANKS, U.S. MARINES

. . .

This kind of insidious threat — the knowledge that there were no front lines, that everywhere was a combat zone — was a hard thing to live with. Day in and day out. The war was with you all the time. For instance, I remember feeling the little tinkle of dog tags around my neck and reminding myself I could go home in a body bag. Because dog tags were in case you were so disfigured they couldn't tell who you were. Yeah, Vietnam had a way of playing on your mind. And it wasn't just the guys in the jungle who felt it. Everyone felt it. I know I felt it, too.

— JUDY JENKINS, U.S. ARMY SOCIAL WORKER

. . .

American soldiers, who had only months before handed out candy to gleeful children, now cast a wary eye on all but the youngest. Anyone could be Vietcong.

. . .

By good acting or good luck, nobody bothered me and when I was completely past the troops and within a stone's throw of the swamp (the direction from which the Viet Cong usually came), I dropped my bucket and peeled off the top two of the three shirts I always wore. The top shirt — the one I would wear all day if nothing happened — was brown. Any Viet Cong seeing it would know that conditions were clear in my sector. The second shirt was white, which I would show if anything suspicious had happened — like a helicopter loitering in the area or a reconnaissance team passing through. The bottom shirt, the one I wore now, was all black and meant that a major threat was around — a fully armed patrol or convoy of troops headed in my direction.

— LE LY HAYSLIP, SOUTH VIETNAMESE CIVILIAN

. . .

...There was this kid, maybe two or three years old. He hadn't learned to walk too well yet, but he was running down the street. And a Marine walked over to talk to the kid, touched him, and they both blew up. They didn't move. It was not as if they stepped on something. The kid had to have the explosive around him. It was a known tactic that they wrapped stuff around kids. The Marine . . . was trying to be friendly.

— ARCHIE "JOE" BIGGERS, U.S. MARINES

. . .

Relentless jungle patrols often meant days of isolation for U.S. troops, followed by sudden combat with an unseen enemy. Weeks of waiting could be followed by a desperate firefight. Their every step was accompanied by the knowledge that a burst of sniper fire could shatter the tense silence and be the last sound they would ever hear.

. . .

When you made contact with the enemy, you went from the most horrible boredom to the most intense excitement I've ever known in my life. You couldn't remain detached. Someone was trying to kill you and you were trying to kill someone, and it was like every thrill hitting you all at once. . . .

— MARK SMITH, U.S. ARMY

. . .

The whole thing was the work of one sniper, who had dug himself a tunnel inside a rice-paddy dike. He had three shooting locations that covered the same killing zone, anybody who walked in there. He shot everybody in the chest. He did no wounding at all. He killed eight people that day. . . . This sniper was shooting only from shoulder to hips. So naturally he was killing everybody he hit. He was a real pro, as good as you're ever gonna see when it comes to snipers.

— JOHN MUIR, U.S. MARINES

. . .

. . . I remember one kid came in completely blown away. He was mute, wild-eyed. What had happened was that he was out on patrol and he was on point. He had lit a cigarette. Then he dropped his lighter. He stooped down to pick up the lighter, and just at that moment a sniper shot at the light and hit the guy in the back of him. So his stupidity had caused this guy to be killed, and he was a basket case, in terrible shape.

— JOHN TALBOTT, U.S. ARMY PSYCHIATRIST

. . .

American soldiers slowly and painfully were making the adjustments necessary to survive a guerrilla war. They learned the things that separated the living from the dead.

. . .

This infantry unit was on a little trail, west of Pleiku, makin' a sweep towards the Ia Drang Valley. This white dude had stepped on a mine. And knew it. He felt the plunger go down. Everybody moved away from him, about 20 meters. So they called for the engineers, and somebody asked for Light Bulb.

I have a nickname from the streets of East St. Louis. Light Bulb. Came from a friend of mine when we were growing up, 'cause he said I was always full of ideas.

When I got there on the chopper, he's been standin' there for over an hour. He really wasn't in any panic. He was very calm. He knew if he alleviated any of the pressure, both of us would have got destroyed.

I dug all around the mine with my bayonet and

found out that it was a Bouncin' Betty. I told him
· I was gonna try to diffuse it. But the three-prong
primer on the Bouncin' Betty had gotten in between the cleats on his jungle boots, so there wasn't
any way I could deal with it. So I said let's see if we
could kind of change the pressure by takin' his foot
out of his boot and me keepin' the pressure by holding the boot down. That way he could get out un-
injured. But when he started doin' that, I thought
I was seein' the plunger rise, so I told him to stop.

I guess maybe I'd been working with him for
maybe an hour now.

Then I got an idea. I knew when the plunger
would depress, the Bouncin' Betty would bounce
up about 3 feet and then explode. So I got the
other members of his team together, and I tied a
rope around his waist. And everybody, including
me, moved off about 20 yards from the mine and
him. And when I counted to three, everyone
would pull the rope and snatch him about 15 feet
off the mine. And it would bounce up its 3 feet
and then explode. And it did that. And the only
damage that he received was the heel of his jungle
boot was blown off. No damage to him

This was somethin' they never taught us in
school.

— HAROLD "LIGHT BULB" BRYANT, U.S. ARMY

·   ·   ·

They always said at OCS, the thing to do with
an ambush is to keep perfectly quiet. To tie up

things so they wouldn't rattle. Not to use rifle slings. To carry a full canteen so the water wouldn't slosh (I didn't think of asking them, "How can I drink? It wouldn't be full anymore.")....

— WILLIAM CALLEY, JR., U.S. ARMY

. . .

You don't walk in no tank tracks, because that's where the bombs are usually. Charlie would use the rationale that most tanks would follow their tracks, and they would booby-trap tank tracks.

— HAYWOOD T. "THE KID" KIRKLAND,
U.S. ARMY

. . .

It's a lot of very small things. . . .

I made my troops wear camouflage on patrol and made them wear helmets and told them I didn't want them smoking. I know they smoked, but I was tough on that because I believed if we were going to stay safe we had to move in the boonies and not be typical Americans, smoking and listening to radios. I remember having a demonstration where I put a helmet out on a flat area, and then I put another helmet out there with branches and stuff on it. It was easy to pick out the helmet without anything on it. I asked, "Which one would you shoot at?" I also did it with people. I put camouflage paint on one guy and all kinds of bushes on his helmet. I put another guy out there, a white guy with no paint and nothing

on the helmet. At about 150 meters you couldn't even see the guy with the camouflage paint. The other guy stood out loud and clear. I said, "Where would you be shooting?" Right for that white face. A lot of people were getting shot in the head. That was a pretty graphic demonstration that you stood a much better chance of getting blown away if you didn't do what you were supposed to do.
— WALTER MACK, U.S. MARINES

. . .

When, for example, we would patrol an area of villages for a number of weeks and continue to lose men to booby traps, and the people in the villages who pretended not to know anything about these booby traps walked the same trails that we did day after day without stepping on them, it became obvious that these people were well informed by the VC where the booby traps were.
— DOUGLAS ANDERSON, U.S. MARINES

. . .

You got to the point where you could smell and feel people around. All your senses were a lot keener. Like your sense of hearing at night. You'd sit out there and it'd be absolutely quiet. You could put a battalion on a hill and hear a pin drop. And as soon as darkness fell, your whole instinct was outside the perimeter. . . . your whole sense of being is out there. You were like living radar.

You also learned to move through dense jungle without making any noise. You move slowly. Stop. Listen. Watch where you put your foot . . .
— JOHN CATTERSON, U.S. MARINES

.   .   .

Should you put your foot to that flat rock or the clump of weeds to its rear? Paddy dike or water? You wish you were Tarzan, able to swing with the vines. You try to trace the footprints of the man to your front. You give it up when he curses you for following too closely; better one man dead than two. The moment-to-moment, step-by-step decision-making preys on your mind. The effect is sometimes paralysis. You are slow to rise from rest breaks. You walk like a wooden man . . . with your eyes pinned to the dirt, spine arched, and you are shivering, shoulders hunched.
— TIM O'BRIEN, U.S. ARMY

.   .   .

And so, day after day, you had dead Marines, wounded Marines, and nobody to fight back at. In the meantime, you've got guys, you know, you go out, you run a patrol, somebody hits a mine and there's a couple of dead people. And here's Joe the rice farmer out in his field. He just, he don't even stop. He don't even, it's like he didn't even hear the blast. And after awhile, you start thinking, well, these people must know where these mines are. How come they never step on them?

They must be, they must be VC. They must be VC sympathizers.

And so, over a relatively short period of time, you begin to treat all Vietnamese as though they are the enemy. If you can't tell, you shoot first and ask questions later.

— WILLIAM EHRHART, U.S. MARINES

. . .

Chapter Ten

search · and destroy

IT WAS AN UNFORTUNATE CHOICE OF WORDS. WHAT IT MEANT
BACK IN 1965, LONG BEFORE IT BECAME UNPOPULAR, WAS
SIMPLY THAT US UNITS OR VIETNAMESE AIRBORNE UNITS AND
MARINE UNITS WOULD PATROL IN THE JUNGLE — NOT IN
THE POPULATED AREAS — TO SEARCH FOR THE MAIN FORCE
COMMUNIST UNITS, FIGHT THEM AND DESTROY THEM.

. . . I COINED THAT TERM. . . . LATER WHEN SOME MARINE WAS
TELEVISED SETTING THE ROOF OF A NATIVE HOUSE ON FIRE WITH
HIS CIGARETTE LIGHTER, THE COMMENTATOR SAID, "HERE'S A
MARINE COMPANY ON SEARCH AND DESTROY," AND FROM THEN
ON BURNING A HOUSE WAS THE "DESTROY" PART OF IT.

— GENERAL WILLIAM DE PUY

GENERAL WESTMORELAND DISAGREED WITH THE STRICTLY DE-
fensive strategy that had prevailed in Vietnam till 1965.
"Search and destroy" operations, Westmoreland argued,
would prove that a good offense is the best defense. By
patrolling the countryside aggressively, U.S. forces could

locate the enemy bases and supply areas and then call in artillery and air strikes.

"Search and destroy" operations were the first step in the new "war of attrition" strategy.

Attrition meant killing the communists faster than they could be replaced. The assumption was that the United States would be able to kill enough of them without suffering significant casualties itself. If a large number of the enemy was killed, sooner or later they would not be able to replace them and the war would be won. To do this Westmoreland needed more men. Privately he voiced his concerns to his commander-in-chief:

· · ·

We are in for the long pull. I see no likelihood of achieving a quick, favorable end to the war.

— GENERAL WESTMORELAND

· · ·

In late July 1965 Johnson agreed:

· · ·

I have asked the commanding general, General Westmoreland, what more he needs to meet this mounting aggression. He has told me. And we will meet his needs. We cannot be defeated by force of arms. We will stand in Vietnam.

— PRESIDENT JOHNSON

· · ·

Johnson not only agreed to send in more ground troops, he also authorized the change in strategy recommended by Westmoreland.

· · ·

... [It] will enable us to find the enemy more often, fix him more firmly when we find him, and defeat him when we fight him. ... Our objective will be to keep the combat tempo at such a rate that the Viet Cong will be unable to take the time to recuperate or regain their balance.

— GENERAL EARLE WHEELER, CHAIRMAN, JOINT CHIEFS OF STAFF

•   •   •

I took my cavalry squadrons and started sweeping over a large area with them. What we'd do is find an area where we thought they'd be or we'd get some clue from the cavalry. Then we'd put at least a battery of artillery down. ... My dad was an artillery man. I like artillery.... I taught ... my guys: Use the biggest thing you can.... There's nothing unfair, if he shoots at you with a rifle, to hit him with a mortar or artillery or even the air force. So when we were searching out there, we'd put the artillery in so it could cover the area of search. If we hit something, *boom*, the big guns were ready.

— HARRY W. O. KINNARD, U.S. ARMY

•   •   •

...I had heard these American generals speak of a war of attrition, but its meaning for the people and the country of South Vietnam had not registered with me. Did [Major General Stanley] Larsen realize that the Viet Cong and the NVA were going to move right back into those hamlets?

84

I asked. "Then we'll go back and kill more of the sons of bitches," he said.

— NEIL SHEEHAN, JOURNALIST

. . .

"Search and destroy" became a term that described all fighting in Vietnam from 1965–1967.

. . .

Then we flew out with the villagers. I think we packed about sixty or seventy Vietnamese in the Chinook, literally one on top of the other. And we took them to a concentration camp. Not like the Nazi version in World War II, where you had ovens and stuff. It was an area with row upon row of these tin shacks. They were packed together, with tin rooves and corrugated aluminum siding. Surrounded by a moat and high fences with concertina wire. At each corner was a watchtower. . . .

— JIM DUFFY, U.S. ARMY

. . .

Now, we realize that you can't go in and then just abandon the people to the V.C. This time we're really going to do a thorough job of it: we're going to clean out the place completely. The people are all going to be resettled in a temporary camp . . . and then we're going to move *everything* out — livestock, furniture, and all of their possessions. The purpose here is to deprive the V.C. of this area for good.

— ALLEN C. DIXON, U.S. ARMY

. . .

We seem to be proceeding on the assumption that the way to eradicate Viet Cong is to destroy all the village structures, defoliate all the jungles, and then cover the entire surface of South Vietnam with asphalt.

> — JOHN MCNAUGHTON, U.S.
> DEPARTMENT OF DEFENSE

. . .

South Vietnamese civilians were now being killed and wounded with regularity. In one incident thirty-one civilians were gunned down while crossing a river in their small boats. U.S. helicopter pilots had mistaken them for Vietcong.

. . .

I don't have nightmares about killing armed soldiers in combat. The thing I have nightmares about is the woman in the rice field that I shot one day because she was running — for no other reason — because she was running away from the Americans who were going to kill her, and I killed her. Fifty-five, 60-years-old, unarmed. And at the time I didn't even think twice about it.

> — WILLIAM EHRHART, U.S. MARINES

. . .

Indeed, the South Vietnamese civilian was becoming the main casualty of the war. The country's cities, especially Saigon, had been transformed by the flood of refugees attempting to escape the destruction of the countryside. One out of every four South Vietnamese peasants had fled ancestral homes and flocked to the cities. Saigon's population had grown from 50,000 to three million. Hundreds of thousands of teenagers now roamed the streets, desperate to make money any way they could.

The war had grown to such proportions that it seemed capable of destroying the whole country. Many South Vietnamese ended up in camps, living in shacks, begging for food, and suffering from diseases caused by the overcrowded and unsanitary conditions created by the war.

Yet, the aggressive new military strategy of search and destroy operations was not enough to stop the enemy's activities. The communists were adapting to U.S. war technology and learning to fight back. They practiced shooting helicopters from the ground, using only rifles. Full-scale mock-ups were constructed in jungle clearings for realistic training. Guerrillas learned to "lead" their target, to shoot where the helicopters were flying to. They learned to calculate the distance based on the helicopter's air speed and angle of approach. Soon the Vietcong were able to predict LZs and therefore use mortar fire and punji sticks effectively. They learned the best time to shoot a slow-moving CH-21 was when it was coming in for a landing.

In one 1967 encounter, communist ground fire downed thirteen U.S. helicopters, killing four and wounding eight. It was a record number of helicopters for a single day.

New kinds of weapons were being used by the U.S. military in Vietnam. Herbicides and defoliants were being used in great quantities. The American strategy was to destroy vegetation (trees, grass, anything that grew) in order to deny the Vietcong a place to hide and thrive. However, this strategy also denied the South Vietnamese peasants a place to live and food to eat. The bombing was now intensified and directed toward this policy of defoliating the South Vietnamese countryside.

· · ·

I had to go back to Tan Son Nhut to catch a C-130 [transport plane] to take me to Cu Chi. On the vehicle going there I met this friend of mine. His name was Captain Denny. Captain Denny wore a chemical sign for his insignia — you know, you wear nurse signs and you wear engineer signs, only he wore the round chemical flask. "What's that?" I asked. "That's the insignia for the Chemical Corps." And I said, "Chemical Corps — what does someone in the Chemical Corps do here?" And he said, "Well, I take care of this herbicide. My mission is to spray and kill the jungle." And I said, "What for?" And he said, "So Charlie can't hide — you know, so it's safer for the troops." And I said, "Oh, my God, how awful to get sent here just to be an exterminator. I mean, if you're going to come to Nam, you ought to come as infantry and kill some enemy. But, I mean, to come and kill weeds—" I felt really bad for him. I told him that, too, and he said, "Yeah, but it's my job."
        — LILY ADAMS, U.S. ARMY NURSE

· · ·

This was an area heavily sprayed with the herbicide Agent Orange. We were not only wading in it, we were eating and drinking it, too. There were lots of particularly hostile forest areas withered away where there were suspected ambush places. But the herbicide planes would also destroy whole crops, rice crops. So we were wading in it and drinking the water.

— JOHN MUIR, U.S. MARINES

. . .

Napalm, a kind of jellied gasoline, was being dropped in large canisters that exploded on impact. The area hit, including humans, was then engulfed in flames. Napalm stuck to everything and attempts to wipe it off only resulted in expanding the area burned. Civilians and soldiers alike were terrified of napalm.

Ia Drang

. . . Someone said to me, "Oh, man, go over to the airstrip. There's a whole pile of boots there. Go get yourself a couple of extra pairs of boots." I was the only one who went across the airstrip to check out the pile of boots. I started noticing men's names in the boots and I said, "Oh, these are somebody's boots. I don't want these boots." Then I noticed piles of fatigues with lots of blood. And then I noticed a couple of . . . boxes, and on the other side of the . . . boxes was my first experience with body bags. . . . I had seen large piles of dead bodies already, VC bodies dropped from a sky

crane for inspection, but I had never seen the
body-bag thing. I had never seen a dead American. It hit me like a ton of bricks because all of a
sudden I realized what the hell was going on and
where they were all coming from. They were
coming from Ia Drang.

— THOMAS BIRD, U.S. ARMY

. . .

In October 1965, American forces, outnumbered four to
one, engaged regular NVA troops in one of the bloodiest
battles of the war.

Some American units were nearly wiped out. The North
Vietnamese fought as close to the American troops as possible, a strategy called "clinging to the belt," in order to
minimize the effect of American artillery and air power.

American and Vietnamese soldiers died side by side, in
one case with hands still gripping each other's throats. Some
fighting took place on hands and knees as machine gun
bullets flew low enough to kill a man crawling on the ground.

In one encounter during the fighting in the Ia Drang
Valley, sixty of one hundred Americans and an estimated
1,700 North Vietnamese were dead.

. . .

By God, they sent us over here to kill Communists and that's what we're doing.

— HAROLD MOORE, JR., U.S. ARMY

. . .

Ia Drang Valley was the first time American and North
Vietnamese had met face to face in a battle. There was no
doubt of the outcome: The Americans had fought well.

The result appeared to confirm Westmoreland's strategy of attrition. To most observers the encounter left no doubt that U.S. military might would prevail in open combat. Ia Drang showed, according to Westmoreland and the Joint Chiefs of Staff, that forcing the enemy into such battles was the surest route to victory in Vietnam.

Up till that time, the war in Vietnam had been fought as a guerrilla war. The hit-and-run tactics favored by the Vietcong guerrillas had not allowed the Americans to use the power of their artillery and air support. The Battle of the Ia Drang Valley was the first major engagement of the war, and Westmoreland saw it as an example of the success of his search and destroy strategy.

Westmoreland's strategy, however, was failing.

. . .

The ability of the Vietcong continuously to re-build their units and to make good their losses is one of the mysteries of this . . . war.
— GENERAL MAXWELL TAYLOR

. . .

The communist leadership in Hanoi had decided to meet the American troop increases with their own. Each year more than 200,000 North Vietnamese reached draft age. The communists decided to accept higher casualty rates and resupply their troops by sending more soldiers down the ever-widening Ho Chi Minh trail into the South, believing that they could kill enough Americans to cause those back in the States to insist that the troops be withdrawn from Vietnam.

. . .

Americans do not like long, inconclusive wars
and this is going to be a long, inconclusive war. . . .

And how long do you Americans want to fight
. . . one year? Two years? Three years? Five years?
Ten years? Twenty years? We will be glad to ac-
commodate you.

— PHAM VAN DONG, PRIME MINISTER,
NORTH VIETNAM

. . .

Chapter Eleven

body · count

IN VIETNAM, THE ONLY MEASURE OF VICTORY WAS ONE OF
THE MOST HIDEOUS, MORALLY CORRUPTING IDEAS EVER
CONCEIVED BY THE MILITARY MIND — THE BODY COUNT.

— PHILLIP CAPUTO, U.S. MARINES

GOVERNMENT OFFICIALS FED THE AMERICAN PUBLIC A MENU
of statistics and newly created military terms that supposedly proved that America was winning the war. There were weapons–loss ratios (they were improving); enemy desertion statistics (they were increasing); kill ratios (we were killing more of them); and, most important, the daily "body count."

Westmoreland insisted the body count proved the U.S. was winning the war, that his strategy of attrition was working. But it wasn't. Not only were body counts in themselves not an accurate indicator of victory, they were thought to be highly exaggerated, and, in a growing number of cases, completely false.

•   •   •

The more regular you were, regular Marine, regular army, the higher the body count was. We had a colonel call in and he was all excited, and he said, "What's the body count, what's the body count?" because we had called in a lot of heavy artillery, we were really putting the job on this one village. So he wanted a real heavy body-count. Well this second Louie we had with us — he'd come up through the ranks — and he yelled, "Over 300." So then the radio man said, "You can't give them an even number. They're not going to go for an even number." So he said "Well, okay, 311." Three hundred and eleven flat out deaths, sure kills. Well this officer loved it. He started yelling "Great, great, you did a great job."

— MATT MARTIN, U.S. MARINES

•   •   •

We ended up fighting the rest of the night. We got three hundred and fifty or sixty of them. The next day you just found their bodies laying all over. General Westmoreland flew in. All the news outfits and everything. It was the most hilarious thing. As these son of a bitches came out there, the GIs started lying. The newsmen would walk up to just anybody and say, "What did you do?" "I singlehandedly killed three hundred thousand with my Bowie knife." And man, they'd write it up.

— HERB MOCK, U.S. ARMY

•   •   •

The daily body count became the yardstick that measured progress in the war. There was great pressure on infantry units to report high body counts.

Officers, eager for advancement, established quotas for units under their command. The soldiers felt that their lives were being risked needlessly. Prisoners of war and Vietnamese civilians were killed and graves were opened to add to the number.

. . .

Some units were given a quota for a week, and if they didn't get it, they were just sent out again.

— RONALD J. GLASSER, U.S. ARMY DOCTOR

. . .

Our . . . Battalion . . . had not been getting the body count that the other battalions in the division had, and General Williamson told that battalion commander . . . that he had better start *producing* or we would get a battalion commander in that battalion that could produce. Colonel Carmichael got the message loud and clear. Approximately two weeks later his fire base was attacked. *He called in that night a body count of 312 and he had taken one wounded.* We flew out the next morning, I flew with General Williamson. . . . We landed and counted the bodies around the perimeter of that base camp, and there were 30-plus North Vietnamese bodies and a few wounded prisoners.

General Williamson questioned him a bit further, and said I understood you have a 312 body count and I see 30-plus here, where are the other bodies? Colonel Carmichael then gave a vague statement of, well I had an ambush patrol in a particular location on the map and they saw 100 Viet Cong moving across an open field that night in preparation for attack and we called in a lot of artillery fire out there, and we counted those 100.

He gave instances like that which amounted to 312. It was obvious to everybody that that was a lie. But General Williamson had put so much pressure on the colonel to produce the body count, the man had no choice. He is forty-five years old and he probably has two kids to send to college, and General Williamson, recognizing that he had placed this pressure on the battalion commander, accepted this lie.

— GREGG HOWARD, U.S. ARMY

• • •

. . . I looked around, and there were about five or six VCs there, shot up. I mean, really torn up something fierce. . . . They were just shot to shit, and two of them were still alive. I turned to my captain and said, "Captain, we got two of them still alive." He said, "So?" I said, "Well, what are we going to do with them?" "What . . . do you think we're going to do with them?" "Do you mean to kill them?" "Yep." It didn't bother me. I just walked over and put a few rounds in their heads. It was like, "Well, hey, he's messed up, and he probably wouldn't live anyway, so I'm just putting him out of his misery." It didn't bother me at all.

— DONALD HINES, U.S. MARINES

.   .   .

Another way, you come across the graves and you call in the number of graves you find. If you come across dead bodies, you count the dead bodies. You resweep the area, recount the numbers, *double it*, and call it on in.

— MICHAEL O'MERA, U.S. ARMY

.   .   .

The "body count" became an ongoing part of the network TV nightly news. But it did little to assure the American public that the ever-widening war would be won, or that it would soon be over. Americans back home were horrified at the mounting toll as more and more of their sons, brothers, and husbands returned home in body bags.

American soldiers were becoming frustrated as the Vietcong often returned within days to villages that had been cleared out at the cost of many lives. There was a growing belief that no territory could be permanently won and that every victory was temporary.

.   .   .

. . . Sending whole regiments out into the hills. Of course, we'd take the territory, then we'd pack up and go home. Two weeks later we could be fighting the same group on the same hill. It never particularly made any sense.

— JOHN CATTERSON, U.S. MARINES

.   .   .

And we weren't gaining any ground. We would fight for a hill all day, spend two days or two nights there, and then abandon the hill. Then maybe two, three months later, we would have to come back and retake the same piece of territory. . . . Two or three months later, we went back to the same area to retake it. We lost 20 men the first time saving it, 30 or 40 men the next time retaking it.

— HAROLD "LIGHT BULB" BRYANT, U.S. ARMY

· · ·

The soldiers found a variety of outlets for their frustration.

· · ·

Our emotions were very low because we'd lost a lot of friends. The death rate was ridiculous for such an operation. So when we went through those hutches, we gave it to them, and whoever was in a hole was going to get it. And whatever was moving was going to move no more — especially after three days of blood and guts in the mud.

— JACK HILL, U.S. MARINES

· · ·

Now, as we skimmed across the paddies, our gunner suddenly opened up with a burst, and a farmer fell down. Later the pilot asked him what he had seen, and the young man, who was very inexperienced, claimed that he had seen the farmer go for a gun. But the pilot and I had been watching too, and we were sure that the farmer had done nothing, that the youngster was nervous.

The pilot reprimanded the soldier, but of course that did not save the farmer somewhere back in the paddies.

— DAVID HALBERSTAM, JOURNALIST

•   •   •

When they came to my house, there were ten family members inside, including my 14-year-old son. Four or five soldiers came right over. When they came in, I stood up and greeted them. They laughed when I did that, they seemed to hate us. They just turned around and threw a grenade into the house. Nine or ten people were blown to pieces. I was the only one who was wounded and survived. My son and everyone else fell dead. I was wounded and extremely frightened and crawled quickly into a corner of the house. Although the grenade had already exploded, the soldiers fired their guns at the people to make sure that nobody would survive.

— LE THI TON, SOUTH VIETNAMESE CIVILIAN

•   •   •

Anyone taking evasive action could be fired upon. Evasive action was never explained to me. It normally entailed someone running or trying to evade a helicopter or any fire. My unit . . . had installed MP sirens on the helicopter and we used these for psychological effect, to intimidate the people. There is one incident I recall where we flew over a large rice paddy, and there were some people working in the rice paddy, maybe a dozen or fifteen individuals, and we passed a couple of times low over their heads and they didn't take any action, they were obviously nervous, but they didn't try to hide or anything. So we then hovered a few feet off the ground among them with the two helicopters, turned on the police sirens and when they heard the police sirens, they started to disperse and we opened up on them and just shot them all down.

— DAVID BRESSEM, U.S. ARMY

• • •

Like I say, you get in the way of an M-14 or M-60 caliber machine gun and there's no tellin' who's gonna get killed. And you get an angry 18-year-old kid behind the gun and he's just seen his buddy gettin' killed. And he's not gonna have no remorse for who's on the receiving end of that 60 caliber machine gun.

— JACK HILL, U.S. MARINES

• • •

By 1967 Pentagon officials were advising the president that the number of men needed in Vietnam would have to be increased to 500,000. The Joint Chiefs of Staff were unable, even at that level, to guarantee a military victory.

Lyndon Johnson felt besieged by a growing antiwar movement in the United States. This controversy was fueled by the mounting number of American dead and wounded, coupled with the absence of any sign of victory. Johnson attempted to end the controversy by making an all-out effort, in the fall of 1967, to convince congressional leaders, the press, and the public that the war was going well.

General Westmoreland was flown back to the United States to help Johnson sell the war. Westmoreland told a joint session of Congress that the U.S. could prevail if those at home continued their support. He appeared confident of victory.

.   .   .

I am very, very encouraged. I have never been more encouraged in the four years that I have been in Vietnam. We are making real progress. Everyone is encouraged.

— GENERAL WESTMORELAND

.   .   .

There had, in fact, been progress militarily: The large American buildup had resulted in a number of battlefield victories. But the war remained at a stalemate.

.   .   .

Before I came out here a year ago, I thought we were at zero. I was wrong. We were at minus fifty. Now we're at zero.

— GENERAL FRED WEYAND

.   .   .

25 Nov 66

Hello dear folks:

It's going to be hard for me to write this, but maybe it will make me feel better.

Yesterday after our big dinner my company was hit out in the field while looking for VC. We got the word that one boy was killed and six wounded. So the doctor, medics and the captain I work for went over to the hospital to see the boys when they came in and see how they were.

The first sergeant came in the tent and told me to go over to the hospital and tell the captain that six more KIAs were coming in. When I got there, they asked if anyone from A Company was there. I just happened to be there, so they told me that they needed someone to identify a boy they just brought in from my company. He was very bad, they said. So I went to the tent. There on the table was the boy. His face was all cut up and blood all over it. His mouth was open, his eyes were both open. He was a mess. I couldn't really identify him.

So I went outside while they went through his stuff. They found his ID card and dog tags. I went in, and they told me his name — Rankin. I cried, "No, God, it can't be." But sure enough, after looking at his bloody face again I could see it was him. It really hit me hard because he was one of the nicest guys around. He was one of my good friends. . . . After I left the place, I sat down and cried. I couldn't stop it. I don't think I ever cried so much in my life. I can still see his face now. I will never forget it. . . .

Love,

Richard

— RICHARD CANTALE, U.S. ARMY

Chapter Twelve

the · war · at · home

OUR BIGGEST PROBLEM IS NOT WITH HO AND WITH THE
FIGHTING OUT THERE. IT'S WITH OUR SITUATION HERE. IT IS
LEADING THE ENEMY TO BELIEVE THAT WE MIGHT QUIT.

— PRESIDENT JOHNSON

AS THE WAR WIDENED AND INTENSIFIED, SO DID THE UNREST at home.

Although the Vietnam War was not their main concern, the organized protest by students and teachers at the Berkeley campus of the University of California in 1964 signaled the beginning of the antiwar movement in America. Six months later, in early 1965, teach-ins were conducted at the University of Michigan and Columbia University in New York City.

At the time, however, the vast majority of Americans still supported the president's policies.

"The Times They Are A-Changin'"

The antiwar movement, begun by college students, was part of a much larger social upheaval. It was called, by

some, a counterculture revolution. Students were reject-
ing many of the traditional values and accepted forms of
behavior that, they believed, characterized the society created by their parents, a society that had become too mate-
rialistic: valuing money and possessions over people.
Society needed change and the students rebelled in a variety of ways, refusing to conform to what was expected of
them.

One form this rebellion took was in the increased use
of drugs, drugs that affected the way students viewed
themselves and their world. Marijuana, called dope, weed,
or grass, was smoked on nearly every college campus.
"Speed" and hallucinogenics like mescaline, peyote, and
LSD, were widely ingested, causing even greater changes
in attitudes as students got high, turned on, and tripped
out.

Not all students participated in the new drug culture,
but many did. And nearly all were affected.

Three army privates refused to go to Vietnam, claiming
that the war was immoral. They were court-martialed and
served two years in jail. Other Americans, feeling deeply
about the war, took even more radical action.

Norman Morrison, a Quaker, set himself on fire in front
of the Pentagon in November 1965. Morrison had been
horrified after he read a French priest's account of the children of his village who had been burned by napalm. Two
other Americans chose to set themselves on fire that year
and both died, one only days after Morrison.

By the fall of 1965 protests were no longer confined to

campuses. Demonstrators took to the streets. More than 15,000 marched outside the White House in late November. Some marchers chanted, "Hey, hey, LBJ, how many kids did you kill today?" which became the anthem of the anti-war movement. More than 100,000 marched in New York City in the spring of 1967, while a smaller, simultaneous demonstration took place in San Francisco. The students were joined by other Americans who opposed the war.

Opposition to the war took a variety of forms: peaceful marches, picketing, demonstrations, prayer vigils, and full-page ads in the nation's newspapers sponsored by prominent Americans.

"We Shall Overcome"

One of the most important aspects of the growing anti-war movement was its link with the civil rights movement.

The war for civil rights was being fought at the same time as the war in Southeast Asia. The acknowledged leader of the civil rights movement was the Reverend Dr. Martin Luther King, Jr.

• • •

Despite feeble protestations to the contrary, the promises of the Great Society have been shot down on the battlefield of Vietnam. The pursuit of this widened war has narrowed the promised dimensions of the domestic welfare programs, making the poor white and negro bear the heaviest burdens, both at the front and at home.

— MARTIN LUTHER KING, JR.

• • •

Ironically, many young black Americans had volunteered to serve in the military to escape the poverty of the ghetto.

Many black leaders viewed the draft as racist. College students could avoid military service, while many blacks and other members of minority groups were drafted in large numbers. Some black leaders urged black Americans to refuse to participate in what they considered a racist war.

. . .

... white people sending black people to make war on yellow people in order to defend the land they stole from red people.

— STOKELY CARMICHAEL, CIVIL RIGHTS LEADER

. . .

By the summer of 1967 racial tension was bubbling to the surface. In the ghettoes of America's cities there were hundreds of racial disturbances and clashes with the police. Twenty-three people were killed in July 1967 during rioting in Newark, New Jersey. Two weeks later forty-three were killed as federal troops were called out to quell rioting in Detroit. There were outbreaks of racial rioting in at least eight American cities.

"All We Are Saying, Is Give Peace a Chance"

By 1967 antiwar demonstrations occurred more frequently, were larger, and had, on occasion, resulted in violence. Antiwar activists were becoming more militant. Campus buildings were seized, ROTC buildings bombed, Selective Service offices forced to close, and induction centers disrupted.

In October 1967 between 50,000 and 100,000 demonstrators went to Washington to participate in the March on the Pentagon. It was the largest antiwar demonstration in the history of the nation's capital. Ten thousand troops were called out. Confrontations erupted and more than 600 were arrested and 47 hospitalized.

These demonstrations caused an angry reaction in those who viewed the antiwar movement as made up of spoiled kids, misguided adults, and traitors. Marchers were attacked with fruits and eggs; antiwar banners were burned. Protesters were sometimes beaten with fists and clubs and occasionally bloodied in confrontations with the police.

Americans were choosing sides: Hawks versus Doves; Hard hats versus Students; Right versus Left; City versus Country; Young versus Old.

Opposition to the war, however, was now coming from a broad cross-section of the American population. Parents began joining their children. A significant number of Americans wanted the war to be over, either through quick victory or equally quick withdrawal. By the end of 1967 polls showed that American support for the war had eroded. Many believed that sending troops to Vietnam had been a mistake and that they should be withdrawn.

The antiwar movement had become a troubling presence. What was once a minority movement on the fringe of American life had, within three years (1964–1967), become a mainstream movement.

In previous wars there had been those who dissented, but the anti-Vietnam War movement became the largest antiwar movement in American history.

This movement was beginning to have an effect on

those young Americans fighting in the jungles and rice paddies of Vietnam.

· · ·

20 September, 1965

Dear Uncle and Aunt,

... Some people wonder why Americans are in Vietnam. The way I see the situation, I would rather fight to stop communism in South Vietnam than in Kincaid, Humbolt, Blue Mound or Kansas City, and that is just about what it would end up being. Except for the fact that by that time I would be old and gray and my children would be fighting the war. The price for victory is high when life cannot be replaced, but I think it is far better to fight and die for freedom than to live under oppression and fear. ...

Your Nephew,

Jack

— JACK S. SWENDER, U.S. MARINES, KIA

· · ·

Tuesday,

November 14, 1967

7:00 P.M.

Dear Mom, Dad, Chris and Vicki,

We were well informed here about the demonstrations by both sides. Even though I'm here, I still have an open mind — realizing, of course, that an immediate pullout or anything of the sort is out of the question. It would degrade the heroic deaths of those who never returned because it would mean going back on everything that we have done. There are many here who feel as I do, but we will continue to fight for the country in which we believe. . . .

Love,
Your son and brother,
Stephen
— STEPHEN W. PICKETT, U.S. ARMY, KIA

•   •   •

10 September '67

David,

. . . Here in Vietnam the war goes on. Morale is very high in spite of the fact that most men think the war is being run incorrectly. One of the staggering facts is that most men here believe we will *not* win the war. And yet they stick their necks out everyday and carry on with their assigned tasks as if they were fighting for the continental security of the United States. Hard to believe but true.

19 October, 1967

Mom and Dad —

. . . It is great to know your family's safe, living in a secure country; a country made secure by the thousands of men who have died for that country.

. . . I have a commitment to the men who have gone before me. . . .

Your son,
Rod
—ROD CHASTANT, U.S. MARINES, KIA

•   •   •

When Americans are talking about Vietnamese

. . . it's not like we're looking at them like they're our next-door neighbors. If someone came to our neighborhood and burned all of our houses and most of our possessions and put us in flying saucers which we'd never seen before and zipped us across the universe, setting us down somewhere in tent city in the middle of a sandbox with wire all around us, I guess we might not be too excited about it. Most of us were never able to see the Vietnamese as real people. . . . I wondered how people would feel in Pittsburgh if the Vietnamese came over in B-52s and bombed them. . . . I'm trying to imagine a bunch of steelworkers after their wives, children, fiancées, parents, grandparents, have been blown up or are running around screaming in agony and some Vietnamese pilot comes swooping down in a parachute. I don't imagine they'd give him a very friendly reception.

— DAVID ROSS, U.S. ARMY

•   •   •

Dear Red,

. . . I have truly come to envy the honest pacifist who honestly believes that no killing is permissible and can, with a clear conscience, stay home and not take part in these conflicts. I wish I could do the same, but I can't see letting another take my place and my risks over here, and the pacifist ideal cannot drive one burning objection to it from my mind: the fact that the only reason pacifists . . . can even live in an orderly society is because someone — be they police or soldiers — is taking risks to keep the wolves away. . . . I guess that's why I'm over here, why I fought so hard to come here, and why, even though I'm scared most of the time, I'm content to be here. At least I'm doing my part according to what I believe.

— GEORGE OLSEN, U.S. ARMY, KIA

. . .

I landed at Travis Air Force Base in California. I did the traditional things, kiss the ground when I got off the plane, and all that. I was so happy that I had survived. And I had a thirty-day leave. It was March 1967.

. . . My brother was living in Berkeley at the time. So I figured I would take a cab to visit my brother before I went back to Philadelphia to see my family. As I'm riding down Telegraph Avenue I told the cab driver that I wanted to walk. It was sunny and beautiful, all these bright colors and people. And the cab driver said, "Are you sure you want to get out here?" Well, of course, I didn't know what was going on. I got out of the cab. I was in my . . . uniform.

I was spit on. This gang of guys walking behind me threw peanuts at me. I went into a bar and phoned my brother. I almost didn't make it out of there. The real shock coming back was in that bar. These guys weren't going to let me out. They wanted to kick my ass. Calling, "You kill any women? You kill any kids?"

These guys were long-haired, long-bearded. And my brother and Nicky and about five other guys came and busted into the bar. There was a big hassle and I stopped them from fighting. I just wanted to get out. My brother drove me to his home and told me what the score was because I just didn't understand. I just didn't know.

We went out to a dance that night. All I had was my . . . uniform. And boy it was such a shock. People looking at me like, "You scum." They'd walk by and spit on the ground. And I got this tremendous feeling that I had done something wrong. It was like I wasn't supposed to have survived.

— FRANK MCCARTHY, U.S. ARMY

. . .

By 1967 public opinion polls showed that Americans no longer trusted Lyndon Johnson. LBJ had become a beleaguered, anguished, and isolated president.

For the first time strong criticism was coming from Congress. Previously, Johnson had been able to pursue his course in Vietnam largely with congressional approval. Now vocal and powerful congressmen were voicing their concerns about the course of the war.

The Senate Foreign Relations Committee had previously begun live, nationally televised hearings on the war. In late November 1967 Senator Eugene McCarthy, who advocated a negotiated settlement of the war, announced he would campaign in the upcoming Democratic presidential primaries. The first was in March 1968 in New Hampshire.

Part Four

The turning point

. . .

1968

Chapter Thirteen

tet

TWO HUNDRED AND THIRTY-TWO GIS KILLED AND 900
WOUNDED MAKES ONE OF THE HEAVIEST WEEKS OF THE
VIETNAM WAR. AND IT IS NOT A WEEK. IT IS JUST OVER
TWO DAYS — THE PAST TWO DAYS. TWO OF THE WORST
WE HAVE KNOWN IN VIETNAM.

— JACK PERKINS, NBC NEWS

Saigon

I'M GOING BACK TO SAIGON AND BE A CIVILIAN IN THE
EMBASSY. NOBODY SHOOTS AT DIPLOMATS.

— GEORGE D. JACOBSEN, U.S. ARMY

. . .

AT 2:47 A.M., JANUARY 31, 1968, A SMALL SUICIDE SQUAD
of Vietcong guerrillas blew a hole in the eight-foot wall
surrounding the American embassy in Saigon.

The United States had just recently decided to place responsibility for the defense of Saigon in the hands of the
South Vietnamese. This was done as a show of confidence.
The four South Vietnamese policemen who had been stationed outside the embassy compound did nothing to help

defend it. One had no weapons, another was asleep, and the other two ran away when the shooting started.

Within five minutes the commando group had killed four Americans, as Marines and military police shot it out with the guerrillas.

Six hours later the embassy was declared secure, but the damage had already been done.

An estimated fifty million Americans watched on television as embassy officials in shirt sleeves and armed with automatic weapons made a room-to-room search. Dead bodies littered the grounds. At one point a pistol was thrown to an embassy official in civilian clothes standing on the second floor. He killed the last of the Vietcong with that pistol.

Seventeen of the nineteen guerrillas involved in the attack were dead. (The two who were captured disappeared after being turned over to the South Vietnamese police.) Seven Americans were dead.

Vietcong guerrillas had secretly entered Saigon in civilian dress, riding bicycles and traveling on buses. Half of the South Vietnamese army was away for Tet, the lunar new year, which was the most sacred holiday of the year in Vietnam. Many of the ARVN who were on duty deserted when the fighting began.

Reports from Saigon provided one of the most incredible scenes ever recorded in the history of warfare.

. . .

. . . we saw the police walking out of a building with this prisoner. His hands were tied and they were taking him down the street. . . .

116

. . . all of a sudden, out of nowhere, comes General Loan, the national police chief. I was about five feet away from him, and I see him reach for his pistol. I thought he was going to threaten the prisoner. . . .

— EDDIE ADAMS, ASSOCIATED PRESS
PHOTOGRAPHER

• • •

The prisoner, who was wearing black shorts and a checkered shirt, had been beaten. Loan waved the soldiers away and, his arm outstretched, aimed his pistol at the prisoner's head.

• • •

. . . So as quick as he brought his pistol up, I took the picture. But it turned out he shot him. And the speed of my shutter . . . the bullet hadn't left his head yet. It was just coming out the other end. There was no blood until he was on the ground — whoosh . . .

— EDDIE ADAMS, ASSOCIATED PRESS
PHOTOGRAPHER

• • •

The photograph appeared on the front pages of American newspapers the next morning. That evening NBC showed an edited film of the shooting. (NBC executives decided to cut the film before the blood began spurting from the prisoner's head.)

• • •

. . . I didn't find this out until much later, but the prisoner who was killed had himself killed a police major who was one of Loan's best friends, and knifed his entire family. The wife, six kids . . . the whole family. . . .

— EDDIE ADAMS, ASSOCIATED PRESS
PHOTOGRAPHER

. . .

The bold attack on the American embassy and the fighting in Saigon were only a small part of an even bolder nationwide offensive.

For the preceding three years both sides had accepted a cease fire during Tet. This time the communists chose Tet to launch the biggest offensive of the war. An estimated 70,000 communists struck every city, town, and major military base in South Vietnam.

. . .

Then the Tet offensive of 1968 broke out, and that was hell. I mean, Charlie was all over the place. He didn't give a shit anymore. He would come out in the open. A bunch of our gunships caught this one platoon of NVA soldiers marching in broad daylight in an open field. They wasted every one of them. Before the Tet offensive, they would sneak around at nighttime. Now they were saying, "We're bad, and we're going to kick your ass."

— DONALD HINES, U.S. ARMY

. . .

The initial thrust caught the American military by surprise, despite signs that it was coming. The CIA had warned the military not to ignore those signs, but the military had disregarded captured documents that indicated the communists were preparing a nationwide attack.

. . .

One of them [spies] . . . had provided us with . . . advance warning of the Communist offensive in 1968, which analysts in Washington unfortunately had ignored.

— FRANK SNEPP, CENTRAL INTELLIGENCE AGENCY

. . .

If we'd gotten the whole battle plan, it wouldn't have been credible to us.

— U.S. ARMY INTELLIGENCE OFFICER

. . .

General Westmoreland and the military hierarchy had believed that the communists had been ground down during the past year and were incapable of coordinating secret, complicated troop movements over a wide area. Westmoreland continued to believe that the main attack would come instead at Khe Sanh, one of the many American firebases in Vietnam. The siege of Khe Sanh, which began ten days before the Tet offensive, on January 20, 1968, continued throughout the days and weeks of the Tet fighting.

Hue

The American military, after recovering from its initial surprise, was able to beat back the communists and inflict heavy losses. Most of the country was reclaimed within days of the Tet offensive. But in the city of Hue, fighting went on for nearly a month. It was the most savage and bloody of the offensive.

. . .

I could feel a knot developing in my stomach. Not so much from fear — though a helluva lot of fear was there — but because we were new to this type of situation. We were accustomed to jungles and open rice fields, and now we would be fighting in a city, like it was Europe during World War II. . . .

My first impression was of desolation, utter devastation. There were burnt-out tanks and trucks, and upturned automobiles still smoldering. Bodies lay everywhere, most of them civilian. The smoke and the stench blended, like some kind of horror movie — except that it lacked the weird music. You felt that something could happen at any minute, that they would jump out and start shooting from every side. Right away I realized that we weren't going to a little picnic.

— Myron Harrington, U.S. Marines

. . .

American soldiers fought street by street while the American artillery attempted to dislodge well-entrenched communists. Nearly every building in Hue was destroyed. Seventy-five percent of the population was left homeless.

Months before the offensive was launched, North Vietnamese leaders had compiled assassination lists. As soon as they took control of Hue, they hunted down those on the list: local leaders, American advisors, foreign doctors, teachers, and missionaries, anyone suspected of associating with the South Vietnamese government.

. . .

We were part of the Hue liberation force in the Tet offensive. The North Vietnamese Army had taken the city . . .

. . . I went into Hue and saw the civilian bodies lined up. I know I didn't kill them. Americans don't shoot people from a distance and then line the bodies up. So when you walk in and find them lined up there on their stomachs with their hands tied behind their backs, you know it was the NVA who did that. . . . They killed the water buffalo, everything.

— ROBERT SANTOS, U.S. ARMY

. . .

As many as 3,000 civilians were believed to have been killed by the communists. Many were beaten and shot and thrown into mass graves. Some were buried alive.

By the end of February 1968 Hue was back in American hands.

Winning the Battle — Losing the War

Westmoreland remained poised throughout the fighting during the Tet offensive. He seemed confident at his appearance during "the five o'clock follies" (as journalists called the official daily briefings given by the military), as he announced that more than 30,000 communists had been killed. So many Vietcong had died, in fact, that it was possible the guerrilla movement in the South had been dealt a crippling blow. The communists had suffered a serious military setback. Although they had taken the Americans by surprise, it was not enough.

The North Vietnamese had been planning the offensive for six months. They hoped that the American defenses could be breached and that the civilian population and the South Vietnamese army would join hands and overthrow the South Vietnamese government. This, the North Vietnamese believed, would force the Americans to withdraw. None of this happened. From a military point of view the Tet offensive failed.

.   .   .

In all honesty, we didn't achieve our main objective, which was to spur uprisings throughout the south. Still, we inflicted heavy casualties on the Americans and their puppets, and that was a big gain for us. As for making an impact in the United States, it had not been our intention — but it turned out to be a fortunate result.

— GENERAL TRAN DO,
NORTH VIETNAMESE ARMY

.   .   .

Once again the United States had won the battle but lost the war, a war watched on television by millions of Americans back home. The size and intensity of the communist offensive shocked the American public. It showed that Johnson and Westmoreland had underestimated the enemy and that the American people had been lied to for the past three years.

The war was not about to end soon. This was going to be a long war, a war in which many more Americans would be wounded or die.

A TV War

What the hell is going on? I thought we were winning the war!

— WALTER CRONKITE, CBS NEWS

. . .

The Tet offensive, by far the biggest battle of the war, was a major news story throughout the world. Saigon was flooded with newspaper and TV reporters, photographers, and film crews.

Television transmitted images of a brutal, expanding war. Scenes of cold-blooded murder, savage house-to-house fighting, the destruction of cities and towns, and young Americans fighting filled America's TV screens. Americans watched television in hopes they could learn what was happening. They had grown to mistrust government officials who appeared to be misleading them purposely.

Perhaps the most trusted and respected person in all of television at that time was Walter Cronkite. "The CBS Evening News with Walter Cronkite" was the most popular news program on television.

Cronkite had been a newspaper wire service reporter during World War II. He was a writer himself, not someone who spoke words written for him by somebody else. Cronkite believed he had a responsibility to report the news as accurately and as fairly as he could. Now, it was becoming clear to him that official government reports were inaccurate.

Stunned by the Tet offensive, Cronkite decided to go to Vietnam to see for himself.

. . .

It was sickening to me. They were talking strategy and tactics with no consideration of the bigger job of pacifying and restoring the country. This had come to be total war, not a counterinsurgency or an effort to get the North Vietnamese out. . . . This was a World War II battlefield. The ideas I had talked about in 1965 were gone.

— WALTER CRONKITE, CBS NEWS

. . .

At ten P.M. on February 27, 1968, nearly ten million people watched Walter Cronkite's special report from Vietnam.

. . .

Who won and who lost in the great Tet Offensive. . . . I'm not sure. . . .

. . . It seems now more certain than ever that the bloody experience of Vietnam is to end in a stalemate.

— WALTER CRONKITE, CBS NEWS

. . .

General Westmoreland believed that negative reporting by the media had turned a military victory into a political defeat. Many agreed.

. . .

I was shocked to find that the Tet offensive, which I had experienced as a tremendous victory in the classical military sense, was somehow being construed by the media as defeat. Aspects of the Tet battle, like the VC penetrating the embassy grounds in Saigon, had been sensationalized. While the fact that we eliminated a good part of the VC infrastructure and decisively dominated them on the battlefield was completely missed by the press.

— KEN MOOREFIELD, U.S. ARMY

• • •

Public opinion at home turned when the average citizen perceived that we didn't know what the hell we were doing. That we had no plan to end the war. And we didn't know what constituted victory. By 1968 the public had given us four years, their money and their sons. So I don't blame the American people. I do blame the national leadership, including the military leadership, for not setting clear and definable goals and objectives.

We had some of our top military leaders appearing before Congress saying, "We're not trying to achieve a victory in Vietnam like Appomattox or World War II." And the obvious question of the guy on the street was, "What the hell are we doing there, then?"

— HARRY G. SUMMERS, JR., U.S. ARMY
GENERAL STAFF, PENTAGON

• • •

By the beginning of March 1968, 2,000 Americans had been killed in the Tet offensive. By the end of the month nearly 4,000 were dead. After Tet the war changed. The war was no longer a guerrilla war; it was a conventional war.

For many Americans the war had not been a question of right or wrong, should we be there or shouldn't we. It was more a question of how long would it take before we won. Tet showed that the answer to that question was "too long."

Chapter Fourteen
khe · sanh

NO SINGLE BATTLEFIELD EVENT IN VIETNAM ELICITED MORE
PUBLIC DISPARAGEMENT OF MY CONDUCT OF THE VIETNAM
WAR THAN DID MY DECISION IN EARLY 1968 TO STAND
AND FIGHT AT KHE SANH.

— GENERAL WESTMORELAND

. . .

MEN, WE HERE AT KHE SANH ARE GOING TO BE REMEMBERED
IN OUR AMERICAN HISTORY BOOKS!

— DAVID LOWNDS, U.S. MARINE BASE

COMMANDER, KHE SANH

KHE SANH WAS LOCATED ON A REMOTE PLATEAU IN THE northwest corner of South Vietnam. The rugged valley that surrounded Khe Sanh was thick with bamboo, twelve-foot-high elephant grass, and other lush vegetation. Frequent low-lying fog along with a dense jungle canopy created a natural camouflage that made detecting enemy movement in the area very difficult.

The Attack

Since 1966 there had been signs of increased enemy activity in the area surrounding Khe Sanh. A year later, Marine search and destroy operations encountered sizable units positioned in the hills surrounding the base. In December 1967 reconnaissance patrols picked up signs of further NVA activity.

. . .

... we heard two clicks from the radio. Someone in the listening post had keyed his own handset twice to tell us he was alive but did not want to talk. I came right back up on the radio and said, "Lima 1-1. Lima 6. If you hear this transmission, key your handset twice."

"Click. Click."

I knew [they] could not talk but that they were listening to me.

"Lima 1-1. Lima 6. When you can talk, let me know what's going on."

And then we waited. The adrenaline went straight through me. I had four Marines out there who thought they saw or heard something. It was darker than pitch. . . .

I was listening so hard I almost missed the faint whisper coming in over my handset. "We see something: Out."

— RICHARD CAMP, U.S. MARINES

. . .

The patrol sightings were supported by intelligence from sophisticated electronic devices. In the fall of 1967 seismic sensors, which activated upon impact, had been dropped into the hills and jungles surrounding Khe Sanh. Other sensors, dropped by parachutes, hung from trees. The sensors picked up troop movements, truck vibrations, even conversations.

A large number of well-equipped NVA troops were surrounding the Marine base. The estimated twenty-thousand enemy force was augmented by armored units and artillery.

General Westmoreland believed that Khe Sanh was of great strategic importance to the American war effort in South Vietnam. It could be used as a base of operations to launch raids on enemy locations and to cut off the Ho Chi Minh trail. Westmoreland increased the number of Marines there and improved and lengthened the airfield.

Rather than abandon the base to the numerically superior force, Westmoreland, banking on American firepower, chose to stand and fight.

·   ·   ·

We are not, repeat not, going to be defeated at Khe Sanh. I will tolerate no talking or even thinking to the contrary.

— GENERAL WESTMORELAND

·   ·   ·

The nearly 6,000 Marines now at Khe Sanh were told to dig in. They dug trenches, built bunkers with roofs supported by wooden beams and covered by sandbags, ran wire with two-inch razor blades on it, fixed trip flares that exploded into a white light that would reveal enemy movement in the dark, and planted thousands of Claymore mines around the perimeter of the camp.

The Siege

On January 21, 1968, the communists began shelling Khe Sanh. The main ammunition dump took a direct hit, and 1,500 tons of explosives detonated. The NVA long-range artillery — some guns were fourteen miles away — struck with deadly accuracy. Seven Marines were killed and four wounded the first day.

. . .

On the morning of January 22, it seemed like everybody was out walking around, assessing the damage and picking up supplies, or whatever. All of a sudden, in the background, I could hear *boomp . . . boomp . . . boomp.* Then someone cried out, "Incoming! Incoming!" I was scared shitless. I frantically searched for cover and dived into a foxhole with another guy. Rounds hit pretty close — close enough. From then on, this became a daily routine. If I was outside, I listened for the *boomp.* This meant that a mortar or rocket or artillery round was about halfway there. I took cover and waited for the round to hit, praying that it didn't have my name on it.

— RODNEY DEMOSS, U.S. MARINES

. . .

29 January 68

Dear Mom and Dad,

I guess by now you are worried sick over my safety. Khe Sanh village was overrun, but not the combat base. The base was hit hard by artillery, mortars and rockets. . . .

I am unhurt. . . . My morale is not the best because my best buddy was killed the day before yesterday. I was standing about 20 feet from him and a 60-mm mortar exploded next to him. He caught a piece of shrapnel in the head. I carried him over to the aid station where he died. I cried my eyes out. I have seen death before but nothing as close as this. Junior, my buddy, had 67 days left in country and then he was to return to his wife and daughter. His death really hit me hard. . . . I feel like an old man now. . . .

Your Son & Marine,
Kevin
— KEVIN MACAULAY, U.S. MARINES

. . .

30 Jan. '68

Dear Ellen,

. . . This is the largest troop movement the NVA has made in the Vietnam conflict to date. They say this battle could be the key to bring Hanoi to the peace table on our conditions.

I guess you might have read about it in the papers. The guys here all have newspaper clippings from home about the mortaring and rocketing of Khe Sanh. That was the worst I've seen since I've been to Vietnam. . . .

Love,
Jim
— JAMES HEBRON, U.S. MARINES

. . .

16 Feb 68

Dear Family,

As you probably already know, we are now at Khe Sanh surrounded by 20,000 NVA troops, so now they can't get away. I never thought incoming artillery sounded so terrible — it just screams out of the sky. . . .

Your Son,

George

— GEORGE STORZ, U.S. MARINES, KIA

. . .

Ground assaults were beaten back, although enemy soldiers got within a few hundred yards of the base perimeter. The Marines, who had been trained to attack not defend, were holding on.

The siege of Khe Sanh was shaping up to be one of the most intense battles of the war. It would be more than two months before the siege ended.

Westmoreland had believed that the enemy's main attack would come at Khe Sanh — that the Tet offensive was only a diversionary tactic.

. . .

Westmoreland thought Khe Sanh was Dien Bien Phu. But . . . Our true aim was to lure your forces away from the cities, to decoy them to the frontiers, to prepare for our great Tet Offensive.

— GENERAL TRAN CONG MAN,
NORTH VIETNAMESE ARMY

. . .

Westmoreland did not believe it.

. . .

The enemy is attempting to confuse the issue. . . . I suspect he is also trying to draw everyone's attention away from the greatest area of threat. . . . Let me caution everyone not to be confused.

— GENERAL WESTMORELAND

. . .

But it was Westmoreland who was confused.

The Tet offensive was over, but the siege at Khe Sanh continued. There were now thought to be between 20,000 and 40,000 North Vietnamese surrounding the Marine base.

Resupplying the base solely by air proved difficult. All food, ammunition, supplies, medical evacuations, and troop replacements had to come in via the airstrip. Enemy machine gun fire and mortars damaged taxiing cargo planes and brought down hovering helicopters. Giant C-130 Hercules cargo planes were unable to perform as expected. Other methods were tried, the most effective being helicopters dangling their loads in nets that hung from their undercarriages. Parachute drops also worked, but they were never enough.

. . .

January 28, 1968

Hi Mom & Dad,

. . . It is bad here, but I don't want you to worry. If you want to know, I'll tell you a little about how I've been living. For the last two days, we went without water and food. Then a chopper came in and we got a couple of meals and about a glass of water for two days. We don't wash or shave. I've got a full beard and no change of clothes. I sleep on the ground, and we get some of our water from the bamboo plants, and eat the roots. We try to catch rainwater and the dew with our ponchos. . . . We get bombarded every day, and at night we get sniper fire. . . . I have lost about fifteen pounds . . . But I'm in real good health. I'm fine and I watch everything I do, so don't worry.

— MICHAEL DeLANEY, U.S. MARINES

. . .

The thing that bothered people the most, I think, was the fact that if you were wounded, you had no assurance that you would be evacuated rapidly. There were several reasons for this. First, the weather often prevented helicopters from landing. Second, even if the birds got in, they sometimes left prior to getting all the casualties aboard.

— WALTER WHITESIDES, U.S. MARINES

. . .

Evacuating the wounded had become a deadly affair. Sick or wounded Marines were used to carry their more severely wounded comrades. This way, when, and if, they reached the helicopters, there would be no return trip through enemy fire — all would climb on board to be evacuated. Acts of heroism and sacrifice became everyday activities.

. . .

. . . For extraordinary heroism . . . On 25 January 1968, Corporal Gomez was the Crew Chief aboard a CH-46 transport helicopter assigned an emergency medical evacuation mission . . . near the Khe Sanh Combat Base. The pilot proceeded to the designated area and landed in the zone as two Marines began leading a casualty, whose head and eyes were covered with bandages, toward the helicopter. When the entire landing zone was subjected to intense enemy fire, the two men were forced to drop to the ground. Observing the blindfolded casualty attempting to reach the aircraft unassisted, Corporal Gomez unhesitatingly left the helicopter and rushed across the 25 meters of fire-swept terrain to the side of the injured man. Quickly pulling the Marine to the ground, he selflessly used his own body to shield his comrade from the hostile fire impacting around them, and as the enemy fire continued, he took cover with the casualty in a nearby rocket crater. Corporal Gomez remained in this exposed area until another crew member rushed to his assistance. Then the two Marines, protecting their wounded comrade from further injury, carried him to the helicopter. The pilot was quickly informed that the injured Marine was aboard, and the aircraft lifted from the hazardous area. . . . Corporal Gomez's heroic actions were instrumental in saving his companion's life and inspired all who observed him. By his courage, selfless concern for the safety of his fellow Marine, and unswerving devotion to duty at great personal risk, he upheld the highest

155

traditions of the Marine Corps and the United States Naval Service.

— NAVY CROSS CITATION FOR
CORPORAL ERNESTO GOMEZ

. . .

Making my way down the trench line I found three of my machinegun crew lying severely wounded. Thinking they had been hit by a mortar shell, I took off my ammunition belt, laid down my rifle and placed one of the wounded Marines on my back. Making my way back through the trench line I suddenly came face to face with an NVA soldier. Instinctively I turned and began running down the trench. . . . The NVA soldier opened fire and I could feel the bullets striking me in the back, but they were not penetrating. The wounded Marine was absorbing the rounds in his flak jacket. I ran right into another NVA soldier who was firing a rocket down the trench line. With the wounded Marine on my back I strangled the NVA soldier with the strap from his rocket pouch. During this incident the young Marine on my back who was now close to death was whispering directions in my ear. Funny, I had started out saving his life, now he had saved mine.

— TOM EICHLER, U.S. MARINES

. . .

At night the Marines waited bracing themselves for the onslaught that was sure to come. By day they repaired perimeter defenses and stayed underground in their bunkers and trenches trying to avoid the enemy shelling. Some took pills to fight diarrhea; too many trips to the latrine could mean death.

• • •

I was going back to the Blue Sector the night of February 11 and I found one of my buddies, Cpl. Dennis Keefe, sitting out on a water can in front of his bunker, polishing his boots. I asked him what he was doing and he told me he was getting ready to go home on a thirty-day leave because he had just extended his tour six months. We laughed about it, that it would probably be over by the time he got back. I told him, "Take it easy and have one for me." As I turned to walk away, I heard a round coming in. When it went off, I fell and a lot of debris and dirt came down on top of me. I turned to check on Keefe, but he was gone. The rocket had hit right where he was sitting. We never found a part of him. No boots, no body parts — nothing.

— FRANK JONES, U.S. MARINES

Operation Niagara

Westmoreland had complete faith in the ability of American firepower to enable the Marines to hold Khe Sanh, even against such overwhelming odds. He personally chose the name for the awesome air attack on the North Vietnamese troops that hid in the hills surrounding Khe Sanh.

• • •

... I gave it the code name NIAGARA to in-
voke an image of cascading shells and bombs ...
carefully co-ordinated round-the-clock shelling
and bombing by all available artillery and aircraft....

In the course of just over two months...
tactical aircraft flew an average of 300 sorties daily
around Khe Sanh, close to one every five minutes, and expended 35,000 tons of bombs and
rockets. B-52's flew 2,602 sorties and dropped
over 75,000 tons of bombs. Marine howitzers
within the combat base and the Army's 175-mm
guns ... fired more than 100,000 rounds, or
nearly 1,500 rounds per day. It was an awesome
display of firepower ... one of the heaviest and
most concentrated in the history of warfare.

— GENERAL WESTMORELAND

• • •

Operation Niagara turned the area surrounding Khe
Sanh into a wasteland. The hills were scorched by napalm
and the constant attacks by 2,000 planes and 3,000 helicopters. The Marines, confident of the accuracy of their air
support, called in air strikes within four hundred yards of
their own positions.

But Niagara could not eliminate the North Vietnamese
artillery. Communist artillery guns remained hidden in
caves until they were about to be fired, then they were
rolled back to avoid detection. Heavy fog added to the
problem — American pilots had great difficulty pinpoint-

ing the enemy artillery. The Marines suffered constant artillery and mortar attack.

As awesome as the American bombing campaign was, it did not save the Marines from frightening, sometimes desperate, hand-to-hand fighting in the hilltop outposts that surrounded the base. Weary Marines fought back the North Vietnamese with knives, fists, grenades, rifle butts, and anything else that allowed them to survive one more day at Khe Sanh.

. . .

. . . I felt around for one of the rifles in the dark. My hand touched an entrenching tool. The spike on it was extended at a 90-degree angle, so I decided it was as good a defense as anything and a better club than a light, fiberglass M-16. I didn't want to shoot unless it was necessary . . . I swung furiously and with all my might.

I was about two feet away from his bare head. He jerked back and my sweaty grip slipped from the handle. He went falling back against the opposite trench wall, with the entrenching tool's spike embedded in his head. . . . He rolled over and lay on the floor of the trench with the spike buried just above his ear. I didn't like looking, but he was making the most bizarre hissing sound that I ever heard another human being make. It sounded like an air hose, and it was nearly as loud. I hoped he was at least unconscious. I pulled the spike out and drove it in again, higher into the side of his head. He quieted, but in a few seconds he was gasping — not moving, just gasping for air. I didn't necessarily want to kill him; I really only wanted to quiet him. I wondered why he wasn't dead after two blows like that into his head. I had never killed a man before, and I couldn't pull out the spike to hit him again with that entrenching tool. It was an overwhelming thing for me to do for the third time. So I left it there, after the second blow, still implanted in the side of his head. I don't think I realized what I had just done.

He was still gasping, but not as much as before. Somehow, I had to quiet him. There was a Marine bayonet a few feet away and I picked it up quickly, trying to decide where to stab him. I was worried about stabbing him in the heart because I didn't know if he could still cry out. After deliberation, I decided on cutting his throat. I asked God to forgive me for what I was about to do to another human being, but then I figured, what the hell, and tried telling myself he was probably going to die anyway and that this was an act of mercy. Besides, he hadn't come onto my hill to discuss peace terms. So I tried cutting his throat. It was impossible. The damn bayonet was as dull as a butter knife. Weren't all bayonets sharp? Next, I tried stabbing and slashing at his throat to open it up. Blood was everywhere. I felt numb. At this point I was a wild man. I was somebody else and yet me. I clicked bone with the blade tip and realized I had torn down into his spinal column. Now he was no longer gasping, but he was gurgling. When was this man going to die? His chest was making wild, frantic heaves, and a haunting, gurgling rattle was desperately respirating out of the gap I had torn open in his throat. Oh God, I thought, please just quiet him down, let him die, for his sake as well as mine. I kept asking myself, Why isn't he dead yet? His gurgling was almost as loud as his gasping had been. It was too much. I had to get away from him. I started down the trench. . . . Then, as an afterthought, I went back to the . . . dying NVA and covered his head with three sandbags, muffling his death rattle. I wondered, why didn't I think of that sooner?

— LAWRENCE SEAVY-CIOFFI, U.S. MARINES

·   ·   ·

But the full-scale attack that Westmoreland expected never came to Khe Sanh. The reason for this is the subject of debate to this day. Westmoreland credited the valiant effort of the Marines, and those who resupplied the base and provided the bombing and artillery support.

By mid-March the North Vietnamese were pulling out.

On March 22, 1968, Lyndon Johnson announced that General Westmoreland would return to the United States, having been elevated to the position of Army Chief of Staff. In June his replacement, General Creighton Abrams, would take over.

On June 17, six days after Westmoreland departed from South Vietnam, Marines began to demolish Khe Sanh. Sandbags were cut open, bunkers blown up, the airstrip dismantled, trenches plowed in, and supplies, vehicles, and ammunition removed. The base at Khe Sanh was being abandoned secretly because the government and military feared the reaction of the American public, a public that had been told just a few months before that their sons and loved ones were defending a crucial combat base. But Khe Sanh was no longer considered crucial.

Ten thousand North Vietnamese soldiers were believed to have been killed at Khe Sanh.

The official count of Marine dead is 205, but that too is the subject of debate. More likely, American deaths were twice that total.

Chapter Fifteen

the · wh●le · w●rld
is · watching

. . . A FEELING IS WIDELY AND STRONGLY HELD THAT "THE
ESTABLISHMENT" IS OUT OF ITS MIND. . . . THAT WE ARE
TRYING TO IMPOSE SOME U.S. IMAGE ON DISTANT PEOPLES
WE CANNOT UNDERSTAND, AND THAT WE ARE CARRYING THE
THING TO ABSURD LENGTHS. RELATED TO THIS FEELING IS
THE INCREASED POLARIZATION THAT IS TAKING PLACE IN THE
UNITED STATES, WITH SEEDS OF THE WORST SPLIT IN OUR
PEOPLE IN MORE THAN A CENTURY.

— JOHN MCNAUGHTON, U.S.

DEPARTMENT OF DEFENSE

. . .

THE WEAKEST CHINK IN OUR ARMOR IS AMERICAN PUBLIC
OPINION. OUR PEOPLE WON'T STAND FIRM IN THE FACE OF
HEAVY LOSSES, AND THEY CAN BRING DOWN THE GOVERNMENT.

— PRESIDENT JOHNSON

206,000

IN LATE FEBRUARY 1968, JUST DAYS AFTER THE TET OFFEN-
sive had been turned back, and while Khe Sanh was

still under siege, Westmoreland had requested 206,000 more men. This would bring the total number of troops to 700,000. Johnson was reluctant to fulfill the request. He turned to his new Secretary of Defense, Clark Clifford, who had recently replaced Robert McNamara.

Secretary Clifford made a thorough review of U.S. war policies in Vietnam. The answers he received from Pentagon officials disturbed him.

· · ·

> How long would it take to succeed in Vietnam? They didn't know. How many more troops would it take? They couldn't say. Were two hundred thousand the answer? They weren't sure. Might they need more? Yes, they might need more. Could the enemy build up in exchange? Probably. So what was the plan to win the war? Well, the only plan was that attrition would wear out the Communists, and they would have had enough. Was there any indication that we've reached that point? No, there wasn't.
>
> — CLARK CLIFFORD, SECRETARY OF DEFENSE

· · ·

Johnson wanted the troop request kept secret, but it was leaked to *The New York Times*. On Sunday, March 10, the story broke on page one: WESTMORELAND RE-QUESTS 206,000 MORE MEN, STIRRING DEBATE IN ADMINISTRATION.

There were those in government who, like many Americans, were puzzled by the request. Why would so large a troop increase come on the heels of Tet, which was supposed to be a resounding victory? If the victory was so great, and the enemy had suffered such terrible losses, why did Westmoreland need 200,000 more men?

Westmoreland and General Wheeler, Chairman of the Joint Chiefs of Staff, explained: The Vietcong had been decimated during Tet. However, they still controlled the countryside. The additional 200,000 troops were needed to allow the American military to regain the initiative that they had before the communists launched their attacks.

Westmoreland's troop request stunned those both in and out of government.

New Hampshire

I am a candidate for the nomination of the presidency on the Democratic ticket. And I run for that office against an incumbent leader of our party, because I believe . . . that we are involved in a very deep crisis of leadership, a crisis of direction and a crisis of national purpose. The entire history of the war in Vietnam . . . has been one of continued error and of misjudgment.

— SENATOR EUGENE MCCARTHY

. . .

The New Hampshire primary is the first primary of each presidential election year. It is closely watched by the media, politicians, and the public. President Johnson's name was not on the ballot because he had not yet formally announced he was running for reelection. But it was assumed he would and would easily win his own party's nomination.

Senator McCarthy's campaign had been going slowly in New Hampshire, despite efforts by his many college-age volunteers. McCarthy's chances were helped significantly by Tet, the siege at Khe Sanh, and *The New York Times* story about Westmoreland's troop request, which ran just two days before the primary.

McCarthy won 42.2 percent of the vote in the primary. He came within 300 votes of defeating the president. McCarthy's surprisingly strong showing was headline news. The New Hampshire results were more an anti-Johnson vote than a pro-McCarthy one and a serious blow to Johnson's already damaged prestige.

Four days later, Senator Robert Kennedy, the younger brother of the immensely popular slain president, entered the race. Kennedy had held back on declaring his candidacy, believing it was nearly impossible to defeat an incumbent president. But now, emboldened by McCarthy's showing, Kennedy announced his candidacy. He and McCarthy, although they did not advocate immediate withdrawal from Vietnam, did represent real opposition to Johnson's policies in Vietnam.

· · ·

... for twenty years we have been wrong. The history of conflict among nations does not record another such lengthy and consistent chronicle of error. It is time to discard so proven a fallacy and face the reality that a military victory is not in sight, and that it probably never will come.

— Senator Robert Kennedy

· · ·

Kennedy's candidacy concerned Johnson. He was the opponent Johnson most feared and most disliked. Unlike McCarthy, Kennedy was capable of winning the national election in November. Polls showed he was more popular than the president.

"I Shall Not Seek"

Lyndon Johnson was, by March 1968, a president hounded from all sides. Opposition to his policies was mounting in Congress. Hawks criticized him for not pursuing the war aggressively. They made it clear that they would not agree to any further troop increases unless a winning strategy was employed in Vietnam. Doves insisted the United States should withdraw from Vietnam.

Johnson was tormented by the course the war had taken. He agonized over the terrible decisions he felt had to be made. Frequently he was unable to sleep at night. At times, wearing his bathrobe, he walked the halls of the White House. He would ask for the latest casualty reports and read the teletype for the latest information on the war.

The country had become bitterly divided in the past year. Security precautions surrounding the president had been intensified. The Secret Service advised Johnson that they believed the climate in the country was so dangerous he should not leave the White House.

All polls showed Johnson's popularity at its lowest point since he had taken office.

At nine o'clock Sunday evening, March 31, 1968, Johnson addressed the nation on network television. He spoke about bringing peace to Vietnam. He announced a freeze in troop levels, a limiting of the air war, and that he would seek to negotiate with the North Vietnamese.

He ended his speech with an announcement that shocked his audience, including members of his own administration.

. . .

> With America's sons in the fields far away and with America's future under challenge here at home; with our hopes and the world's hopes for peace in the balance every day, I do not believe that I should devote an hour or a day of my time to any . . . duties other than the awesome duties of this office — the presidency of your country. Accordingly, I shall not seek, and I will not accept, the nomination of my party for another term as your President.
>
> — PRESIDENT JOHNSON

. . .

Three weeks after the New Hampshire primary Martin Luther King, Jr., was assassinated, shot while on the balcony of a Memphis, Tennessee, motel. Spontaneous rioting erupted in Boston, New York, Chicago, Detroit, and a hundred other cities. There was a fear that American cities might be overrun by the upheaval triggered by the sudden killing of the nation's most respected black leader.

Two months later, on June 5, Robert Kennedy was shot on the evening of his victory in the critical California primary. A three-and-a-half hour operation failed to save his life and he died the next morning.

Chicago

Senator McCarthy continued his campaign. However, by the time the Democrats arrived in Chicago for their convention, Vice-President Hubert Humphrey was thought to be the likely nominee.

Humphrey had done nothing to separate himself from Johnson's war policy. This earned him the support of Johnson and the power brokers in the Democratic party, who favored the obedient Humphrey over candidates like McCarthy, whom they considered radical. Humphrey's near-certain nomination left large segments of the Democratic Party feeling that they were not represented by the process in Chicago. They considered the convention "fixed."

The convention delegates had widely different and strongly held views on the war, reflecting how deeply divided the Democratic Party had become because of Vietnam. There was bitter debate over the Party's position on the war, but Johnson, controlling the convention from behind the scenes — and aided by his loyal vice-president — made sure the convention did not adopt an antiwar position.

The large and vocal antiwar delegations from New York and California were seated at the back of the hall. During important debates and floor fights their microphones were turned off. On the convention floor tension and physical confrontation were the order of the day. Delegates who disagreed with the Johnson/Humphrey forces were, at times, physically escorted off the floor. But as heated as the atmosphere inside the amphitheater was, the violence that was flaring up outside overshadowed it.

Ten thousand demonstrators had come to Chicago;

some came to protest peacefully, but most came to disrupt the convention by any means necessary. For months there had been rumors and stories about what would happen in Chicago, including rumors that as many as 100,000 people might come to Chicago. But the threat of possible violence, among other factors, kept many away. Those who did come were, to some degree, the more radical elements of the antiwar movement.

Richard Daley, the mayor of Chicago, vowed to maintain security. All 12,000 Chicago police were working twelve-hour shifts as the convention got under way. Six thousand national guardsmen were called out. Aircraft were restricted from flying over the amphitheater where the convention took place.

Those who came to Chicago were aware of the potential for violence.

As soon as the convention began, there were ugly clashes between the demonstrators and the police. On the evening of August 28 demonstrators overran police barricades and headed for the Hilton Hotel, where most of the convention delegates were staying. They were blocked by the police and national guardsmen in jeeps strung with barbed wire. The crowd verbally taunted the police and chanted "the whole world is watching." Television cameras had been going back and forth between the continuing confrontations on the convention floor and the freewheeling violence in the street. Now, as blood was about to flow in the streets of Chicago, the events outside took center stage at prime time.

Under orders from Mayor Daley, the police, having removed their identification, charged the crowd, swinging their nightsticks and chanting "kill, kill, kill" as they eagerly attacked the crowd. The police, joined by the national guardsmen, were indiscriminate, beating and clubbing demonstrators, radicals, activists, and troublemakers, along with convention delegates, newsmen and photographers, and innocent bystanders. One group was forced through a plate-glass window, which cut them as they fell through. The violence spilled into the streets of downtown Chicago, as the police and guardsmen beat demonstrators with clubs and rifle butts and the dispersing crowd retaliated with bottles and rocks.

McCarthy's convention offices were turned into a field hospital that tried to help the 800 who were wounded. Convention delegates who attempted to come to the aid of those cornered by police were themselves beaten.

While the full-scale "police riot" (as federal reports later called it) was taking place outside, Hubert Humphrey was winning the nomination inside.

Three weeks before the Democratic convention the Republicans had nominated former vice-president Richard Nixon.

During the campaign Nixon promised to bring the war to an honorable end, implying that he had a plan to end the war and would unveil it when he was elected.

On November 5, 1968, Nixon defeated Humphrey and was elected the thirty-seventh president of the United States.

Part Five

Peace with honor

. . .

1969–1975

Chapter Sixteen

a · nightmare · war

In Vietnam the best army the United States ever put
into the field is numbly extricating itself from a
nightmare war. . . .

— Robert Heinl, Jr., author of
The Collapse of the Armed Forces

"Vietnamization"

Richard Nixon planned to shift responsibility for the ground war to the government and army of South Vietnam. This policy became known as "Vietnamization." American troops were to be withdrawn in planned phases, while the South Vietnamese army was to be built up. ARVN forces were to be increased, and in 1969, 150,000 men were added, bringing the total to one million. The United States was to supply the South Vietnamese with equipment, materiel, and arms — including helicopters and more than a million M-16's. America would continue to supply supporting air power, including B-52 bombing strikes.

In June 1969 Nixon announced that 25,000 troops would be withdrawn. Further withdrawals were announced in September and December. By the end of the year only 479,000 American military men and women were in Vietnam — the lowest number since 1967.

Despite the announced troop withdrawals, the war dragged on. In 1969, 9,414 Americans died.

The knowledge that back in the States the political leaders had decided that it was time to hand the war back to the South Vietnamese only complicated the lives of the Americans who had to continue to fight. Vietnam continued to be a place where death might be just a shot away. "Don't be the last American to die in Vietnam," communist radio warned U.S. soldiers. The warning was unnecessary.

· · ·

When Johnson rolled out and Nixon came in . . .

The emphasis became "Let's get the damn thing over. Let's close it out, with as much dignity as we can, but let's just back off and come home." And that permeated all the way down to Snuffy in the field. Not just my guys, but Boonie Rat out there with a commissioned unit. It became a matter of survival then. . . . Because we knew by then that we were going to come out of there.

— GARY RIGGS, U.S. ARMY SPECIAL FORCES

· · ·

I think the major aim of anybody over there at the time was just to take care of himself. The main objective was just to live through it. . . .

— BOBBY MURDOCH, U.S. MARINES

· · ·

Fragging

By 1969 morale had fallen to a dangerously low point. There was a widespread breakdown in discipline. Soldiers in Vietnam were aware that they were fighting an unpopular war. New arrivals came bearing the antiwar sentiment that was spreading back home. Antiwar literature was readily available in Vietnam.

Troop withdrawals were good news to those going home. To those remaining it meant they might have to die for a cause nobody cared about anymore.

. . .

By every conceivable indicator, our army that now remains in Vietnam is in a state approaching collapse, with individual units avoiding or having refused combat, murdering their officers ... drug-ridden and dispirited where not near-mutinous.

— ROBERT HEINL, JR., AUTHOR OF
THE COLLAPSE OF THE ARMED FORCES

. . .

Prior to 1969 the premeditated killing of American officers by their own troops was rare. Statistics were not even available. But beginning in 1969 there was an average of 240 attempts a year — and those are the documented cases.

The killing of an officer by his own troops was called "fragging." "Fragging" got its name from fragmentation grenades, which were used because they were destroyed along with the target in the explosion. A grenade could simply be rolled into an officer's tent and the officer blown to pieces. Grenades, however, were not the only weapons used to kill unpopular officers.

. . .

. . . A friend of mine put sixteen rounds in a staff sergeant's back in Vietnam. The staff sergeant received a Purple Heart, was put in a green bag and packed home. No autopsy or anything else.

The staff sergeant was just an incredibly short-tempered, evil man. They would go out humping for eighteen days, come home, and he'd hold a full field inspection or some shit. You had to un-load, clean your weapon, stand a full field inspec-tion, and you only got three hours' sleep that night. That's what I'm talking about, you see. Sleep is the most valuable thing in the world over there. If anybody . . . with your sleep, you want to take their asses off.

— JAMES HEBRON, U.S. MARINES

. . .

. . . There were some associates of mine who were experiencing some problems from a gun-nery sergeant: he was an older guy, a career man, gung-ho. He liked the war; he was very petty in terms of how Marines should be dressed, even in a war zone, and he made sure that everything was spit and polish and he just generally made a nui-sance of himself. At one point the company was out — they'd gotten pinned down by the enemy. When they found the gunnery sergeant there were more holes in his back than in his front, so that would lead one to believe that some of his own men made every attempt to kill him too.

— CHARLES JOHNSON, U.S. MARINES

. . .

That night, the captain came over. This was Captain Chicken Shit. He said, "I want you to take your squad to the listening post up there." This was around six-thirty, seven o'clock at night, and you could hear the gooks jabbering away out there. I said, "I ain't taking my men out there." By this time, I was a nervous wreck. I had lost Hill with the short artillery round. Two days before, a guy named Hank and another guy had joined my squad. Both of them were hit. I had lost three of my own guys that day . . . I was shaking like a leaf, and he was saying, "You're going to take your squad out there. . . ." I said, "No, I'm not," so he left. Our lieutenant came over and said, "The captain wants us to go over there." I said, "I am not taking my guys out. You can hear them. They're not more than ten yards in front of us." "I know, I'll try to talk to the captain about it." He went back, and I heard them arguing. The lieutenant came back with the captain, and the lieutenant was saying, "I don't want to send them out." The captain said, "I told you to get your squad together and get out there, and you're going to do it right now." I just pulled out my .45, and pointed it to his head. I said, "Before I go out, sir, I will blow your . . . brains out." He turned

beet red and turned around and walked away.
The lieutenant said, "Don't worry about it." I said,
"I'm not."

— DONALD HINES, U.S. MARINES

. . .

There were rewards ranging from $50 to $1,000 for the
killing of certain officers. A $10,000 bounty was placed on
one officer's head, for ordering an attack on "Hamburger
Hill," so-called because so many Americans were ground
up in the attack. (Miraculously, he survived the war.)

More than 1,000 Americans died as a result of fragging.

Drugs

Drugs had become another pervasive and serious problem. Thousands — it would soon be as many as 20,000
Americans — had to be hospitalized because of addiction
or hepatitis caused by dirty needles. Drugs could be gotten
as easily as gum or cigarettes, and it was estimated that half
of those fighting in Vietnam were smoking marijuana,
while one third of the men stationed there, according to
official reports, were thought to be addicted to heroin or
opium.

. . .

The majority of people were high all the time.

— FRED HICKEY, U.S. ARMY

. . .

"GI, you want Vietnamese cigarette? I trade
you one pack of Salem." . . . For a box of Tide, you
could get a carton of pre-packed, pre-rolled marijuana cigarettes soaked in opium. For ten dollars

you get a vial of pure heroin about . . . the size of . . . a cigarette butt. And, you could get liquid opium, speed, acid, anything you wanted.

— GEORGE CANTERO

. . .

I had to be totally tuned up. We were doing Dexedrine. When we'd go out on a mission, we'd take a whole handful of pills. . . . When I hit Dexedrine I'd just turn into a pair of eyeballs and ears, That's probably why I don't remember too many of the details real well, because it was just like I was on a speed trip the whole time I was in the field.

— MIKE BEAMON, U.S. NAVY

. . .

Bloods

Racial conflict between blacks and whites was now part of life in Vietnam, just as it was back in "The World."

. . .

The racial incidents didn't happen in the field. Just when we went to the back. It wasn't so much that they were against us. It was just that we felt that we were being taken advantage of, 'cause it seemed like more blacks in the field than in the rear.

In the rear we saw a bunch of rebel flags. They didn't mean nothing by the rebel flags. It was just saying we for the South. It didn't mean they hated blacks. But after you in the field, you took the flags very personally.

— RICHARD J. FORD III, U.S. ARMY

. . .

The racial polarization was deeper there than I've ever seen. They had black sides of town and white sides of town. . . . And woe to the white who walked in a black area unaccompanied, and vice-versa.

— SGT. RALPH THOMAS

. . .

There was no question that a barrier had sprung up between black and white soldiers. For example, blacks had their own club in the battalion base camp. Whites were not welcome there. I think blacks felt alienated and isolated. They were finding it harder and harder to identify with this war. Back in the United States, before they ever came into the army, the Black Power movement was emphasizing their differences. This was a "white man's war, not a black man's war."

— KEN MOOREFIELD, U.S. ARMY

. . .

. . . I had some trouble with a racist lieutenant from Miami. He called me a ". . . Puerto Rican." I got in a fight with him and he gave me an Article 15. I told him — when there weren't any witnesses — "Don't ever think about putting yourself in front of me in a firefight, because I'll blow your head off." After that he never turned his back to me. In combat you can kill anyone. A lot of people died that way.

— ANGEL QUINTANA, U.S. ARMY

In the Rear

American soldiers were going AWOL (Absent Without Leave for less than thirty days) and deserting (AWOL for more than thirty days) in increasing numbers. There were reports of mutinies by entire companies. In 1969, 117 American soldiers were convicted of refusing to follow orders, forty more than in 1968.

The army responded to the morale problem by issuing medals. But so many medals were issued (in 1970, a half a million — nearly two for every American stationed in Vietnam) that they ceased to have meaning for many soldiers. Medals were referred to as "gongs," and one medal was handed out so often that it came to be called a "rat turd."

Resentment was growing between those "humping the boonies" and those stationed in the rear, away from the fighting.

. . .

April 20, 1969

To: THE PRESIDENT OF THE UNITED STATES, COMMANDER-IN-CHIEF OF THE UNITED STATES ARMED FORCES

. . . I think it is necessary to explain to you that basically there are two different wars here in Vietnam. While we are out in the field living like animals, putting our lives on the line 24 hours a day, seven days a week, the guy in the rear's biggest problem is that he can receive only one television station. . . . The man in the rear doesn't know what it is like to burn a leech off his body with a cigarette; to go unbathed for months at a time; to sleep . . . in a foxhole; to walk all day on feet raw from immersion foot; or to wake up to the sound of incoming mortar rounds and the cry of your buddy screaming "Medic!"

— YOUR FIGHTING MEN IN VIETNAM:
(SIGNED BY THIRTY SOLDIERS)

Sgt. Edward F. Noonan
Sgt. Alfred D. Seaman
Sp/4 Fredrick R. Bagwell
Sp/4 Steve Ivey
Sp/4 William H. Tross
Sp/4 Bruce Joel Dunham
SP/4 Charles P. Harang
PFC Raymond L. Williams
PFC James J. Lindsay
Sgt. Phillip J. Boyenga
Sp/4 David W. Campbell
PFC Andrew Norton
PFC William I. Purnell, Jr.
PFC David A. Bild
PFC Gary H. Thole

PFC Charles W. Fletcher
PFC Jay William Rech
PFC Gary L. Stull
PFC David F. Ney
PFC Clark Williams
PFC David B. Anderson
PFC Bruce M. Applegate
PFC Clyde Beckham, Jr.
PFC Daniel T. Erickson
PFC Thomas J. Hatte
PFC Thomas J. Jordan
PFC Glenn E. Holland
PFC Gary C. Schneider
Sgt. Robert R. Rudesill
PFC Dennis G. Foell

• • •

Officers too often directed combat operations from helicopters and command posts safe from harm.

• • •

I have been in situations in Vietnam where an infantry platoon or company was fighting on the ground, trying to attack across an open rice paddy

164

in the hot sun of the day. The battalion commander and his operations officer were sitting in a
helicopter at a thousand feet. The brigade commander was at fifteen hundred feet. The division
commander was at twenty-five hundred feet. The
corps commander was at three thousand feet. . . .

Now, I can assure you from the point of view of
some infantry man who is down there sweating his
ass off, facing hot lead at very close quarters, it's
very difficult to respect or identify with his leadership sitting up in the clouds in starched fatigues.
— KEN MOOREFIELD, U.S. ARMY

· · ·

The people in Washington setting policy didn't
know what transpired over there. They were listening to certain people who didn't really know
what we were dealing with. That's why we had all
those stupid restrictions. Don't fight across this
side of the DMZ, don't fire at women unless they
fire at you, don't fire across this area unless you
smile first or unless somebody shoots at you. If
they attack you and run across this area, you
could not go back over there and take them out. If
only we could have fought it in a way that we had
been taught to fight.
— ARCHIE "JOE" BIGGERS, U.S. MARINES

· · ·

There were areas you weren't supposed to fly
over. There were areas where if you took fire you
had to call back maybe all the way back . . . to the

commanding general of the division to get permission to fight, to fire back, and that to me was
absurd. We're fighting a war. Somebody's shooting at you. You turn around, you shoot back and
you kill him.

— FRANK HICKEY, PILOT

. . .

The constant and complicated restrictions on how the
war could be fought had been a frustration for Americans
fighting in Vietnam since the war began. But by 1969 these
frustrations had reached a peak. The American soldier in
Vietnam in 1969 was, among other things, lonely, tense,
frustrated, and young.

Nothing illustrated this more clearly than the revela-
tions of the massacre at My Lai.

My Lai

If we learn to accept this, there is nothing we
will not accept.

— JONATHAN SCHELL, JOURNALIST

. . .

In the first three months of 1968, Charlie Company lost
five men because of mines, booby traps, and snipers.
Twenty-three more had been seriously injured. They had
yet to see the enemy. After being out on patrol for weeks,
the soldiers were tired and tense. Many of them were looking forward to meeting the Vietcong face to face. They had
learned to hate the Vietnamese. All Vietnamese.

. . .

This was a time for us to get even. A time for us
to settle the score . . . when we can get revenge
for our fallen comrades.

— KENNETH HODGES, U.S. ARMY

· · ·

The men of Charlie Company were preparing to attack
the area surrounding the small hamlet of My Lai, which
had a population of about 700 people. Lieutenant William
Calley was to lead an advance patrol into the area the
morning of the attack.

· · ·

I was — I guess hyper is the right word. I think
I would say keyed up. And my mind was psychologically set to do battle. I was tense and nervous.
I was definitely hyper. I had tremendous amounts
of adrenalin flowing through my body. I had an
abundance of energy from just the basic excitement of everything, or the emotional fear of going
into combat to meet a superior force.

— WILLIAM CALLEY, JR., U.S. ARMY

· · ·

Two hundred and fifty Vietcong were believed to be living and operating in the area surrounding My Lai. On
March 15, the night before the attack, Calley and his men
were given final instructions by Captain Ernest Medina,
the Commanding Officer. Captain Medina's instructions on
the eve of battle are still the subject of debate.

The soldiers assumed the landing zone would be "hot"
but, surprisingly, Calley's platoon met no resistance.

· · ·

The majority of us had expected to meet VC combat troops, but this did not turn out to be so. First we saw a few men running . . . and the next thing I knew we were shooting at everything. Everybody was just firing. After they got in the village, I guess you could say that the men were out of control.

— DENNIS I. CONTI, U.S. ARMY

. . .

Calley and his men, over the next four hours, brutalized and savagely murdered more than five hundred old men, women, children, and babies.

The Army took no action on the information it received about this incident, including eye witness accounts from survivors.

. . .

It is the responsibility of all military personnel having knowledge or receiving a report of an incident or of an act thought to be a war crime to make such incident known to his commanding officer as soon as possible. . . .

— A 1968 U.S. MILITARY DIRECTIVE

. . .

There was no attempt to investigate the activities at My Lai.

The American public knew nothing of the events of March 16, 1968, until late in 1969, when the story began to break in the media. At that time the massacre at My Lai became a sensational international news story.

On November 17, 1970, the court martial of Lieutenant William Calley began. He was charged with premeditated murder. His defense was that he was just following orders given to him by his superior, Captain Medina.

. . .

> I was ordered to go in there and destroy the enemy. That was my job that day. That was the mission I was given. I did not sit down and think in terms of men, women and children. They were all classified the same, and that was the classification that we dealt with, just as enemy soldiers . . . I felt then and I still do that I acted as I was directed, and I carried out the orders that I was given and I do not feel wrong in doing so.
>
> — WILLIAM CALLEY, JR., U.S. ARMY

. . .

On March 29, 1971, the jury found Lieutenant Calley guilty of premeditated murder. He was sentenced to life imprisonment.

The verdict and sentence were highly controversial and provoked an outpouring of support for Calley.

Some of those who opposed the war saw him as a small part of an even larger evil: The war itself was immoral, not the men forced to fight it. Calley was taking the blame while his superiors escaped responsibility. Many Americans saw little difference between Calley's killing of innocent civilians and decisions made every day to bomb and napalm villages. Others thought that things like this happened in every war.

* * *

My Lai was not an isolated incident . . . only a minor step beyond the official United States policy in [Vietnam].

— AL HUBBARD, EXECUTIVE SECRETARY, VIETNAM VETERANS AGAINST THE WAR

* * *

The biggest stink I heard when I was there was over the My Lai stuff. That happened because the guys who went in there were wearing uniforms. They had on their name-plates . . . everybody was outraged. On a lot of operations we weren't even allowed to wear dogtags.

— YOSHIA CHEE, U.S. ARMY SPECIAL FORCES

* * *

In November, 1974, Lieutenant Calley was paroled.

Chapter Seventeen

the · madman

I CALL IT THE MADMAN THEORY.... I WANT THE NORTH
VIETNAMESE TO BELIEVE THAT I'VE REACHED THE POINT
WHERE I MIGHT DO ANYTHING TO STOP THE WAR. WE'LL
JUST SLIP THE WORD TO THEM THAT, "FOR GOD'S SAKE, YOU
KNOW NIXON IS OBSESSED ABOUT COMMUNISTS. WE
CAN'T RESTRAIN HIM WHEN HE'S ANGRY — AND HE HAS HIS
HAND ON THE NUCLEAR BUTTON."

— PRESIDENT RICHARD M. NIXON

RICHARD NIXON'S VIEWS ON VIETNAM WERE NOT, IT TURNED out, much different from those of his predecessors. Like Truman, Eisenhower, Kennedy, and Johnson, he was committed to denying the communists control of Vietnam.

President Nixon believed that victory in Vietnam was possible. Like Johnson he had faith in the ability of U.S. bombing to demonstrate American military power. While withdrawing ground troops, he also intensified and expanded the war, determined to show the North Vietnamese that he was willing to take steps that Johnson had considered too risky. In fact, Nixon wanted the communist leaders to think he was irrational and, hence, capable of anything — a madman.

Cambodia

President Nixon chose Cambodia, Vietnam's western neighbor, as the first step in creating his "madman" image.

In early 1969, without consulting Congress, Nixon authorized the secret bombing of Cambodia. The targets in Cambodia were resupply bases used by the Vietcong and the North Vietnamese Army. They contained supplies, fuel, training and truck repair facilities, and hospitals, and served as a jumping-off point for attacks into South Vietnam. The communists had been using these sanctuaries since the war began.

Fearing that knowledge of this action would ignite antiwar protests, the operation was kept secret from the American public. Previously the American military had not been allowed to strike into neutral Cambodia.

· · ·

We knew that the American commanders had strict orders . . . to respect the Cambodian border. That's why we abused Cambodia's neutrality. Whenever we were chased by the enemy, we knew we could retreat across the frontier . . . into the safe zone and get some rest. We were protected by international law. Also, we knew there was a large antiwar movement in America who would not allow the American army to cross over the border.

— NGUYEN TUONG LAI, VIETCONG

· · ·

To maintain the strict secrecy of the Cambodian missions, an elaborate system of double reporting was used.

The bombing plan was code-named "Operation Menu" and continued for over a year, with each segment named for a different meal: Breakfast, Lunch, Dinner, etc. Those who directed the flights were ordered to falsify their records.

The pilots and navigators of the B-52's were officially briefed on targets inside South Vietnam, near the Cambodian border. Some, however, were privately informed that they would be attacking different targets in the morning — targets within Cambodia. All paperwork having to do with the strikes was burned. Officially, the illegal bombing of Cambodia did not occur.

·   ·   ·

In the event press inquiries are received following the execution of the Breakfast Plan as to whether or not U.S. B-52s have struck in Cambodia, U.S. spokesman will confirm that B-52s did strike on routine missions adjacent to the Cambodian border but state that he has no details and will look into this question. Should the press persist in its inquiries . . . U.S. spokesman will neither confirm nor deny reports of attacks on Cambodia but state it will be investigated.

— GENERAL EARLE WHEELER, CHAIRMAN,
JOINT CHIEFS OF STAFF

·   ·   ·

The results of Operation Menu, like those of Rolling Thunder, were disappointing. Communist troops were not eliminated — they simply drove deeper into the interior of Cambodia. As they did, the B-52 strikes followed. An unknown number of Cambodian civilians were killed. The enemy, however, was still able to operate out of the sanctuaries in Cambodia.

In early 1970 Nixon decided to take an even bolder step. On April 30, with the public still unaware of Operation Menu, he announced he was sending ground troops into Cambodia.

. . .

Tonight, American and South Vietnamese units will attack the headquarters for the entire Communist military operation in South Vietnam. This key control center has been occupied by the North Vietnamese and Vietcong for five years in blatant violation of Cambodia's neutrality.

This is not an invasion of Cambodia.

— PRESIDENT NIXON

. . .

Kent State

The invasion of Cambodia took the American public by surprise. Vietnamization seemed to be proceeding as planned, and ten days earlier, Nixon had announced another large troop withdrawal. The war was no longer dominating the network's nightly news and seemed to be winding down. Now what seemed like a move to expand, not end, the war had been announced.

The heavy volume of mail to the White House mostly opposed the invasion, and the nation's newspapers ran sharply worded editorials denouncing the action. Two hundred State Department employees signed a petition to voice their opposition to the decision publicly.

The invasion provoked widespread protests. Antiwar

demonstrations erupted in the streets within hours of Nixon's televised address. On May 1 students at Kent State University in Ohio demonstrated against the war, breaking windows, setting fires, and damaging cars as the demonstration turned into a riot.

The next night the Kent State ROTC building was burned to the ground. The governor of Ohio called out the National Guard and vowed to preserve order. On May 4 the students again gathered. They were asked to disperse but refused, throwing rocks at the national guardsmen who had surrounded them. The National Guard responded with tear gas. One of the guardsmen, thinking he had heard a gunshot, opened fire. Others joined in. When the volley was over, four students lay dead and fourteen others injured.

The nation's colleges and universities erupted in the wake of the Kent State killings. Two hundred schools were forced to shut down and hundreds were disrupted by protesting students. More than 75,000 demonstrators converged on Washington. Buses were placed around the White House and troops deployed in anticipation of a possible attack.

Kent State rocked the nation. Many Americans, however, blamed the students, not the authorities, for the violence. The White House and other political leaders had little sympathy for rioting antiwar protesters.

· · ·

They're the worst type of people we have in America.

— JAMES RHODES, GOVERNOR OF OHIO

. . .

...when dissent turns to violence, it invites tragedy.

— RON ZIEGLER, PRESIDENTIAL PRESS SECRETARY

. . .

If it takes a bloodbath, let's get it over with.

— RONALD REAGAN, GOVERNOR OF CALIFORNIA

. . .

A month later Nixon announced that the invasion had been a success. But this was not completely true. The invasion did result in the capture of thousands of enemy troops as well as weapons and supplies. But the enemy was still able to operate out of the sanctuaries in Cambodia.

The Paris Peace Talks

We all went and stayed in a hotel room rather than renting apartments or finding other kinds of accommodations. It didn't occur to any of us at the time that five or six years later there would still be a delegation in Paris going over very much the same ground.

— JOHN NEGROPONTE, U.S. DELEGATE,
PARIS PEACE TALKS

. . .

...We could have got out of the war in a year, if we really set our minds to it. We were in it another seven years. We lost another 20,000 men.

— CLARK CLIFFORD, SECRETARY OF DEFENSE

. . .

Richard Nixon believed that the communists were counting on the antiwar movement to force him to withdraw from Vietnam. He was not about to withdraw, however, without an agreement he considered acceptable.

The Paris Peace Talks had been taking place since May 1968. At first the talks were stalemated over questions of where they would be held and who would participate and where delegates would sit.

Finally it was agreed that the representatives of the United States, the governments of both South Vietnam and North Vietnam, and the South Vietnamese communists would sit at a circular table. None of the negotiating parties would have any flags or other kinds of identification. This settled after eight months, the talks proceeded to other, more substantive, disagreements.

The United States wanted mutual withdrawal of North Vietnamese and American troops from the South. The North refused, demanding that the United States remove its troops immediately and unconditionally. The North Vietnamese also made it clear that negotiations would proceed more rapidly if the United States would abandon the South Vietnamese government. The North Vietnamese wanted South Vietnamese President Nguyen Van Thieu to resign. Thieu had disagreed strongly with the decision to include the South Vietnamese communists, the Vietcong, in the talks and had refused to attend sessions for several days. By April 1969 the talks had reached a stalemate, as each side continued to make demands the other would not accept.

In July 1969 President Nixon proposed that the United

States and the North Vietnamese negotiate secretly. The North Vietnamese agreed and talks got under way in February.

. . .

> We'd usually go on a Saturday morning, drive out to Andrews air force base to a special hangar . . . get on the plane, fly across the Atlantic all day Saturday, and land in central France, get out and transfer to a small French jet . . . and fly from there to the outskirts of Paris where we'd be met by our military attaché at the Embassy who had rented a car under an anonymous name; drive to a safe haven apartment to get a night's sleep, negotiate with the Vietnamese on Sunday and with the time change we could fly back late Sunday and still go in the office the next morning as if nothing had happened.
>
> — WINSTON LORD, U.S. DEPARTMENT OF STATE

. . .

After more than four years of sporadic talking, the negotiations had yielded nothing.

Then, toward fall 1972, there was movement. The United States, via the Soviet Union, informed the North Vietnamese that it was willing to bend on its insistence on mutual withdrawal. The North Vietnamese indicated that they might be willing to allow Nguyen Van Thieu, the president of South Vietnam, to remain in power.

In October 1972 the North Vietnamese further recommended that they and the United States settle all military matters, establish a cease-fire, work out troop withdrawals, and prisoner exchanges, etc. The South and North Vietnamese governments would settle all political questions.

The October 1972 North Vietnamese proposal ended the stalemate.

The negotiations were completed and the text was agreed to and set for the signing on October 31, 1972.

Despite Nixon's promise of support, Thieu refused to sign. By mid-December, the talks had collapsed.

The Christmas Bombing

Earlier in the year, in March 1972, the North Vietnamese had launched a major offensive. One hundred twenty thousand NVA soldiers, backed by hundreds of Soviet tanks, artillery, and equipment, drove into the South.

ARVN troops fell back as the communists attempted to capture as much territory as possible. With American troop strength down to 100,000, the time seemed right. The North Vietnamese hoped that these moves on the battlefield would improve their position at the negotiating table.

President Nixon responded to the offensive by authorizing Operation Linebacker I. Linebacker I was the first use of B-52's over North Vietnam since 1968. The bombing continued for nine months. Nixon also announced that all major ports in North Vietnam would be mined to prevent supplies from coming in by ship.

.   .   .

I think the North Vietnamese had exhausted themselves temporarily in the '72 offensive. I think they had shot their bolt for a while. They took quite a few casualties ... the American bombing . . . was certainly extensive. There were these on-again, off-again peace feelers, and then Nixon said, "Okay, guys, we're going to mine the harbors and we're going to blow the shit out of you people.". . .

I think the effect of the mining of the harbors . . . was that the North Vietnamese were afraid of Nixon. They didn't know what he was going to do. . . .

— BRUCE LAWLOR,
CENTRAL INTELLIGENCE AGENCY

.   .   .

By the summer the North Vietnamese offensive had been stopped by the American bombing. Military and civilian casualties on both sides had been heavy.

In November 1972 Richard Nixon had been reelected in a landslide victory. Nixon carried every state in the Union except Massachusetts.

After the election, a confident President Nixon decided that a show of strength was needed to force the communists back to the bargaining table. Nixon gave the North Vietnamese an ultimatum: negotiate or suffer the consequences. They had seventy-two hours to respond.

On December 18, 1972, Nixon's deadline, he authorized Linebacker II, the heaviest and most concentrated bombing of the war. The sustained bombing was intended to intimidate the North Vietnamese. Nixon did not place the limits on the bombing that Johnson had, all military and economic targets were fair game: Roads, railways, power plants, radar installations, fuel depots were all pounded by the B-52's in eleven days of bombing. Much of the bombing took place over heavily populated areas in the North. The North Vietnamese evacuated one third of the civilian population of Hanoi — 500,000 people.

The American press was highly critical of the bombings, which some called barbaric because of the intense nature of the bombing and the Christmas timing. Countries normally supportive of U.S. actions also voiced their disapproval. The Americans were accused of needlessly striking civilian targets to create an atmosphere of terror: hospitals and residential areas in which hundreds of innocent civilians were killed. The Americans denied the charges.

Although the Christmas bombing was a controversial decision, the North Vietnamese did, as a result, return to the peace talks.

On December 30, 1972, the bombing was stopped.

On January 8, 1973, Nixon informed Thieu that the United States was prepared to sign a separate peace agreement with the North Vietnamese.

On January 20, Richard Nixon was inaugurated for a second term as president of the United States.

On January 23, one day after Lyndon Johnson died, a cease-fire agreement was initialed.

On March 29, 1973, the last American troops left Vietnam. The direct involvement of the American military in the war in Vietnam was over.

· · ·

We have finally achieved peace with honor.

— PRESIDENT NIXON

· · ·

But some questioned that.

The issue over which the war was fought — the status of the government of South Vietnam — was left unsettled.

More Americans died during the peace talks than in all previous years of the war: 15,315 between 1969 and 1972. Despite the troop reductions, 4,300 Americans died in 1972 alone. Over 100,000 South Vietnamese and 400,000 communists were killed. Civilian deaths are estimated to have been, during that same period, in excess of 750,000 people.

The End

Neither side obeyed the agreement arrived at in Paris.

South Vietnamese troops attempted to seize as much territory as possible. The heavily outnumbered North Vietnamese sent nearly 100,000 men down the Ho Chi Minh trail to reinforce their ranks in the South.

By the summer of 1974, ARVN troops, no longer protected by American soldiers, were vulnerable to attack by the North Vietnamese. They were strategically spread thin, ammunition was scarce, and military logistics poor. Morale, always a problem, resulted in nearly 250,000 men deserting in 1974 alone. That year 80,000 Vietnamese — North and South — were killed — the highest total for any year in the war.

By December 1974 the North Vietnamese were planning what they hoped would be their final offensive. Troop strength had been increased to 285,000 men. The highways and pipelines they had built were in place. Their earliest hopes for victory was 1976, but most considered that optimistic.

The North Vietnamese struck hard and fast. By January 6, 1975, they were sixty miles north of Saigon.

President Thieu ordered his generals to withdraw and form a new line of defense further south. But the South Vietnamese government made no announcement of these plans. Rumors spread and a sense of panic set in. Thieu's commanding general simply flew away from the area. Junior officers were left to coordinate the withdrawal. Hundred of thousands of civilians were left to fend for themselves.

On March 25, 1975, the North Vietnamese took Hue without any resistance. A million civilians, remembering the 1968 Tet massacre, fled the city. Four days later, Danang, South Vietnam's second largest city, also fell. Thousands of terrified citizens left Danang heading for the coast. Whole ARVN divisions deserted, many trying to return home to help their families. Some South Vietnamese soldiers shot civilians in order to save themselves. Others took off their uniforms hoping to be considered civilians by the conquering communists.

By the end of March the strategic withdrawal had become a military disgrace. By April, two-thirds of South Vietnam was controlled by the communists.

.   .   .

Why, it's like a goddam circus parade gone haywire! The elephants have moved out in front and everybody else is stumbling through their shit.

— THOMAS POLGAR,
CENTRAL INTELLIGENCE AGENCY

.   .   .

In Danang people were going absolutely ba-
nanas. I remember nothing but mass hysteria —
people hanging off the wings of airplanes. . . . The
roads were jammed. It was almost impossible to
get anywhere. This was the end of March, 1975.

. . . I'm . . . on a refugee barge . . . There were
all these hundreds of people trying to get on the
barge. People pushing each other off. Mothers losing babies overboard. People throwing possessions
over, throwing each other's possessions over, people coming up in rafts and getting pushed off by
people who were on the barge. . . .

— JULIE FORSYTHE, THE AMERICAN FRIENDS
SERVICE COMMITTEE

. . .

President Thieu was outraged by the Americans' refusal
to intervene. He asked Graham Martin, the new American
ambassador, for more aid. Martin assured Thieu that he
would get it. President Gerald Ford, who had succeeded
Richard Nixon on August 9, 1974, after Nixon resigned because of the Watergate scandal, asked Congress for more
money. But Congress, accurately reflecting the mood of
the country, refused the request. Thieu, bitter, remained in
the presidential palace, refusing to take calls from his field
commanders.

By the beginning of April there were still thousands of
Americans in South Vietnam: embassy officials, military
personnel, American businessmen and women, charity
workers, and others. Slowly they were being evacuated.

Forty thousand NVA troops were only thirty-five miles from Saigon. On April 21 Thieu resigned, denouncing the United States in a televised speech for abandoning his country. He was believed to have taken several tons of gold with him when he left the country four days later.

As late as April 29 U.S. Ambassador Graham Martin refused to begin the evacuation of Saigon. He feared that a rapid evacuation would cause panic. Those Americans still in Saigon had to be evacuated as well as thousands of South Vietnamese (and their families) who had worked for the Americans and were likely to be killed if left behind.

The North Vietnamese were on the outskirts of the city, shelling the airport. Hysteria was spreading.

The speed with which the South Vietnamese army collapsed seemed to take Ambassador Martin by surprise. He appeared blind to the fact that the war was coming to an end. This delay contributed to the chaos as the last Americans left South Vietnam.

The original evacuation plans had to be scrapped, as desperate crowds blocked buses and jammed the streets.

On April 29, 1975, all Americans were ordered to leave Vietnam. At 3:00 P.M., helicopters began the final evacuation. In less than twenty-four hours 1,000 Americans and nearly 6,000 Vietnamese were taken from Saigon rooftops. The helicopters shuttled between the city and the decks of American aircraft carriers waiting offshore. One helicopter crashed, killing two crewmen. They were the last Americans to die in Vietnam.

All the Americans were evacuated but thousands of

Vietnamese remained. Some, fearing what would happen to them because they had worked for the Americans, committed suicide.

An estimated 10,000 Vietnamese flocked to the U.S. Embassy. Ambassador Martin, ill with pneumonia, was led to the roof at 4:45 A.M. on April 30, 1975. He held the now-folded American flag that had flown over the embassy.

Frantic Vietnamese attempted to break through the locked gates or scale the embassy walls. They were beaten back by Marines using their rifle butts. Thousands were left behind as the last American helicopter lifted off and headed out to sea.

That morning, at 7:30 A.M., North Vietnamese tanks began to enter the city.

Chapter Eighteen

coming · home

IT WAS A WAR WE SHOULDN'T HAVE BEEN IN — WHICH EVERY-
BODY, MILITARY AND NONMILITARY, SAID THE SAME THING. WE
DIDN'T HAVE ANY REASON FOR BEING THERE. BUT THE FACT
WAS WE WERE THERE, AND WE DID THE BEST WE COULD.

— PINKIE HOUSER, U.S. ARMY

POWs

DURING THE 1972 CHRISTMAS BOMBING, FIFTEEN B-52'S were shot down by the North Vietnamese, ninety-three airmen were lost, and thirty-one captured. They were the last American POWs.

In 1964 Lt. Everett Alvarez, Jr., had been the first.

· · ·

... I was very low, just skimming the trees at about five hundred knots. Then I had the weirdest feeling. My airplane was hit and started to fall apart, rolling and burning. I knew I wouldn't live if I stayed with the airplane, so I ejected, and luck-ily I cleared a cliff.

— EVERETT ALVAREZ, JR., U.S. NAVY
(POW 1964–1973)

· · ·

Alvarez went down while flying a mission immediately following the Tonkin Gulf incident in August 1964. He was sent to an old French prison, where he was held in captivity for eight years.

The prison walls were four feet thick, twenty-five feet high, and topped by electrified barbed wire. The Americans called it the Hanoi Hilton.

. . .

I was shot down on the twenty-eighth of June, 1967, and I was released on the third of March, 1973.

. . . I was shot down by antiaircraft. . . .

I was in an F-4 Phantom in a squadron and was hit at twelve thousand feet going in excess of five hundred knots. That's really quite a shot. . . .

. . . and then I had to think about getting out . . . so I went ahead and ejected myself. . . .

. . . I landed in a rice paddy, up to my waist in water. I looked around and on the bank of this rice paddy was a militia guy waiting right there for me. . . .

. . . and they took us right up to Hanoi. . . .

It wasn't until Hanoi that the real brutality occurred.

They kept us blindfolded and would not allow us to speak. If we tried to speak they would hit us with the butt of a gun. . . . We had our hands tied; escape was virtually impossible because we were so well guarded. We disrobed right down to our skivvies and we were barefoot. . . .

The collection point for the first arrivals was the central Hanoi prison. It was called Hoa Lo. It's a famous prison that goes back to colonial times, probably built by the French before the turn of the century, and it occupies an entire city block in Hanoi . . . people tend to call that Hoa Lo complex the Hanoi Hilton.

— WILLIAM LAWRENCE, U.S. NAVY
(POW 1967–1973)

. . .

They took me to the prison camp we called the Hilton first for the first extensive interrogations. That's where they had the torture room and can put the screws to you. When I had mentioned the Geneva Convention, they laughed in my face. They said, "You're not qualified to be treated as a prisoner of war. You're a criminal. . . ."

. . . they put me in a concrete cell that was about 6 by 9 feet. You either had a board or a concrete pallet for a bed. And, at first, you were told to sit on it all day. If they saw you moving around, trying to exercise, or trying to communicate with somebody, then they would beat you.

— NORMAN ALEXANDER MCDANIEL,
U.S. AIR FORCE (POW 1966–1973)

. . .

In those days one guy tended to do most of it. I think they learned that if they didn't have a guy who was reasonably skilled at doing the torturing, it was really easy to kill somebody. . . . They fundamentally wanted to keep us alive because they knew we had hostage value. . . .

Basically our camp had seven-foot-square cells . . . Many of us were in solitary confinement . . . I spent fourteen months in solitary confinement in one of those cells.

— WILLIAM LAWRENCE, U.S. NAVY
(POW 1967–1973)

. . .

Captured Americans had been confined to small cells, containing only a bed and bucket. Rats and insects were all over, and the prisoners were given little to eat. Injured or ill POWs were usually not given medical aid. Escape was unlikely, if not impossible, and survival the first order of the day.

. . .

You learn very early that you had to do certain things. First of all, you learned that you had to have a positive outlook, you just couldn't feel sorry for yourself, and I think that all of us went through a period of "Why me?" where you went over the mission many times and said, "Gee, if I'd done this differently I would have avoided getting shot down." I think that was the common tendency — to refly your mission a hundred times — and then the full reality of the situation dawned on you, that you were in prison and were likely to be there for a long time with little likelihood of being able to communicate with your family. It was obvious to me after I'd been there for several weeks that they weren't going to allow me to write home or receive mail. So after about a month or so, you realize that you're in there for a long time and you are cut off from the outside world and you are relying purely on your own resources to pull you through. And that's when I started developing some kind of disciplined type of thought process and exercise program. . . .

. . . For example, I said, "Okay, I'm going to try to resurrect the names of as many kids as I can in my first grade class." I'd dwell on that for hours and hours and hours. Then I'd start on the second-grade class. It was amazing. I think I relived my life in minute detail three times. I think it took about two weeks to go through my whole life, of about eighteen hours a day of very intensive thought. It was amazing how many names out of my first grade class I could resurrect.

. . . you had to develop a positive outlook: "I'm going to keep myself as healthy mentally and physically as I can. I'm going to have to live a day at a time and make the best out of each day." And you got to the point that you no longer spent hours fantasizing or thinking about your family or thinking about the future. You lived that day, that activity that you were in at the time. Your world really got small, but you had to do that. I would get so wrapped up in a particular project that I'd be completely oblivious to anything else. . . .

I also exercised every day . . . And I always

forced myself to eat everything they gave me . . . I figured that if you ate everything they gave you, you'd probably have around fifty to one hundred calories. Over a period of years we slowly kept progressively losing weight. I lost about forty pounds. . . .

— WILLIAM LAWRENCE, U.S. NAVY
(POW 1967–1973)

. . .

POWs were subjected to constant physical and psychological torture aimed at getting them to confess their crimes. Some were tied with ropes that pulled their limbs from their joints.

The debate on the degree of resistance to North Vietnamese torture grew bitter and divided American POWs. Some, called diehards, believed in resistance up to the point of death or permanent injury. Others resisted, but not as rigidly. Some cooperated with the North Vietnamese because of the pain and fear, others because of a sincere belief in the antiwar statements they gave. These statements were often filmed for propaganda purposes. One POW blinked the Morse code for "torture" while giving his "confession." Those who did cooperate had to be kept separately from the majority of the POWs.

. . .

Here's where one could get into a discussion about the Code of Conduct. It says you're not supposed to give them any information or write any statements, all that stuff. But the code is just a guideline. In 1955, President Eisenhower signed this executive order — which is not law — that became the Code of Conduct.

— JERRY DRISCOLL, U.S. AIR FORCE
(POW 1966–1973)

. . .

When questioned . . . I am bound to give only name, rank, service number and date of birth. I will evade answering further questions to the utmost of my ability. I will make no oral or written statement disloyal to my country. . . .

— U.S. MILITARY CODE OF CONDUCT

. . .

. . . Well, for a while people said you've got to observe it absolutely, word for word. But in Vietnam you quickly realized that you couldn't physically do it. Or you're dead. Some can take it more than others, but everybody's got a breaking point. Or else, you may not break but you're also very dead. Because they're not going to stop. I guarantee you. They . . . will . . . not . . . stop, period.

— JERRY DRISCOLL, U.S. AIR FORCE
(POW 1966–1973)

. . .

I don't know of a case where an individual didn't give something. It may or may not have been the absolute truth, but I'd be almost willing to bet that everyone gave at least something through torture, and only through torture. [Even so,] it eats away at you and you are mortified.

The feeling you betrayed your country, I think, was a common feeling amongst every one of the POWs.

— RICHARD MULLEN, U.S. NAVY (POW)

• • •

Many POWs developed a profound hatred for the American antiwar movement. They believed that while they endured daily deprivations and hardships, those back home were acting like traitors.

• • •

One way they conducted psychological warfare was to show us reports from *The New York Times*, the *Washington Post*, news magazines, and the *Congressional Record*, displaying the antiwar sentiments at home. It was hard to drive ourselves on day after day when the guards showed us the newspaper stories of protestors flying the VC and North Vietnamese flags around the Washington Monument, while students burned American flags.

The interrogator . . . would say, "Look, this is your Capitol. Look where our flag is, look where your flag is. Why do you resist, your own country looks at the people who support our cause as heroes. Why do you stay here and suffer?"

— DAN PITZER, U.S. ARMY SPECIAL FORCES
(POW 1963–1967)

• • •

Actress Jane Fonda was particularly resented by American POWs. Fonda was an outspoken antiwar activist who, in the summer of 1972, visited North Vietnam for two weeks. She went to hospitals, schools, factories, and villages struck by American bombs. She was filmed applauding the North Vietnamese soldiers who manned an antiaircraft gun that was used to shoot down American planes and shown after she climbed aboard one and looked down the sights. She also volunteered to make antiwar statements over Radio Hanoi.

. . .

This is Jane Fonda speaking in Hanoi, and I'm speaking particularly to U.S. servicemen who are stationed in the Gulf of Tonkin.

You are very far away, perhaps, and removed from the country you're being ordered to shoot shells at and bomb, and the use of those bombs, or the condoning of the use of these bombs, makes one *a war criminal.*

The men who are ordering you to use these weapons are *war criminals* according to international law, and in the past in Germany and Japan, men who were guilty of these kinds of crimes were *tried and executed.*

— JANE FONDA, ACTRESS

. . .

Her speeches were broadcast to the American POWs inside the Hanoi Hilton.

. . .

It was worse than being manipulated and used. She got into it with all her heart. She wanted the North Vietnamese to win. She caused the deaths

of unknown numbers of Americans by buoying
up the enemy's spirits and keeping them in the
fight.

— GEORGE DAY (POW)

· · ·

She was filmed with American prisoners who told her
they were well treated, never tortured, and wanted the
United States to withdraw from Vietnam.

· · ·

They [the POWs] assured me that they were in
good health. When I asked them if they were
brainwashed, they all laughed. Without exception
they expressed shame at what they had done.

— JANE FONDA, ACTRESS

· · ·

She appeared not to realize that the POWs had been
forced to say statements written for them by the North
Vietnamese. She was not allowed to visit the Hanoi Hilton.

Nor was she aware that prisoners who refused to appear
with her were tortured or that one pilot who refused was
rumored to have been killed.

After the 1968 bombing halt, and the death, a year later,
of Ho Chi Minh, the treatment of American POWs improved.

· · ·

We think there are a couple of reasons for the
torture stopping. Ho Chi Minh had just died the
month before. We think the new leaders had a
change in policy about the POWs. He was more
harsh, absolutely. The guy was ruthless, abso-

lutely ruthless. But the people who came afterward may have realized, Hey, we're not gonna win this war outright. Something's gotta give. And they knew we were more valuable alive than dead. . . . North Vietnam was very worried about world opinion, so we think that helped.

— JERRY DRISCOLL, U.S. AIR FORCE
(POW 1966–1973)

. . .

. . . But the thing that really made us get our hopes up was when the B-52s came in and bombed Hanoi. Christmas '72. That's when we knew that the attitude among the North Vietnamese had really changed. We could see it in the guards, in the officials that we saw in the camp. The B-52 bombing . . . they changed from cocky confidence to a desire to get the war over. I could see it. They were tired of fighting. After so many years of sacrifice and deprivation, now the war was being brought to the heartland. I think that's when we started to say to ourselves, "It's just a matter of time."

— WILLIAM LAWRENCE, U.S. NAVY
(POW 1967–1973)

. . .

The return of all Americans held by the North Vietnamese was one of the central issues at the Paris Peace Talks; 2,000 airmen had been killed, thousands were missing in action (MIA), and more than six hundred had been captured.

By April 1, 1973, all acknowledged POWs were released into American hands.

. . .

It was a very emotional time. They brought us to the airport in six buses. Two buses per airplane. So here I am in bus five. When we first pulled up at Gia Lom airport, I could see the C-141. The first two buses went. The plane started taxiing out, and then it stopped because the second 141 came in and landed. It taxied in, and the first one took off. We're standing in the bus, and we started yelling. The guards were trying to keep us quiet, but we didn't care. It was real, it was really happening. Up to then we didn't believe it, even though we were in civilian clothes. They had given us these jackets and slacks and these tight, pointed Italian shoes.

The second airplane filled up, taxied out to the runway and took off. We're looking. There's still two buses. I was thinking to myself, Oh shit. It was deathly quiet for the longest time. Maybe twenty minutes, maybe five. Nothing. No sounds. Finally somebody said, "Hey look up there!" Sure enough, the third 141 came down the runway and landed.

We lined up . . . They called out my name. I stepped forward. There was a colonel. I saluted him and said, "Good to be back." He shook my hand and said, "Congratulations, glad to have you back." We stepped another twenty feet and there was another colonel. I saluted him. He turned me over to an air-crew member, who escorted me to the 141. He had to hold on very tight to my arms, because I was so emotional. . . . I was all choked up. . . . As I got closer and closer to that 141, I looked up at the tail and saw a big red cross painted on it. On top of that red cross was a big, beautiful American flag.

— JERRY DRISCOLL, U.S. AIR FORCE
(POW 1966–1973)

. . .

Heroes and Heroines

PFC Willett covered [his] squad's withdrawal, but his position drew heavy enemy machine gun fire, and he received multiple wounds. [He] struggled to an upright position and, disregarding his painful wounds, he again engaged the enemy with his rifle to allow his squad to continue its movement and to evacuate several of his comrades who were by now wounded. Moving from position to position, he engaged the enemy at close range until he was mortally wounded.

— CONGRESSIONAL MEDAL OF HONOR CITATION
FOR LOUIS E. WILLETT, U.S. ARMY, KIA

. . .

. . . As I became closer to some of the Marines, I could get them to work with me on the casualties. They would give me cover fire when I needed it. They knew very well how to take care of their corpsmen. There was no lack of cover fire and there was usually a fire team with me when I went after a casualty. There were several occasions when I did have to go out alone, which were the most horrifying experiences I've ever had in my life....

... They knew if they got hit that I would come after them. I wouldn't just lay back there and cry. I would come get them.... And I know that if I had been hit and there was no way to get out of there, they would have grabbed me up in a poncho and carried me a hundred miles if they had to. There was that kind of feeling. This was above and beyond any kind of politics.

— DOUGLAS ANDERSON, U.S. MARINES

. . .

One thing I want to say — those medics and those nurses performed feats that I can't describe in any other way than to say they were heroic. If the war had any true heroes, they were the medics and the nurses.

— ANNE ALLEN, JOURNALIST

. . .

While fighting in Vietnam, 47,253 Americans were killed. Ten thousand four hundred forty-nine others died of other causes. Three hundred twelve thousand six hundred sixteen were wounded — half of them seriously. The large number of wounded was the result of two factors. Each of these factors, in their own way, came to characterize the war in Vietnam.

First, the enemy used booby traps, mines, and ambushes — the weapons of a guerrilla war. Although they could be deadly — and often were — they tended to

wound and maim. Twenty percent of the American injuries were from booby traps and mines.

Second, and more important, the improvement in available medical facilities resulted in thousands of lives saved.
Many of those wounded in Vietnam would have died in
other wars. The art of battlefield medicine was never practiced more efficiently than in the jungles, mountains, and
rice paddies of South Vietnam.

Helicopter crews frequently braved enemy fire in their
attempts to land and take the dead and wounded aboard.
Medevacs — medical evacuations — by helicopters lifted
casualties from firefight to field hospitals at speeds of 165
mph or more.

.   .   .

The Army likes to pride itself that no one hit in
Nam is more than ten minutes away from the
nearest hospital. Technically they're right. Once
the chopper picks you up, it's a ten-minute ride to
the nearest surg or evac facility. . . .

If you're going to die in Nam, you'll die straight
out, right where it happens.

If you don't die right out you've got a pretty
good chance; the evac and surgical hospitals do
anything and everything . . . In Nam if they take
you off the choppers alive, or just a little dead, it
may hurt a lot but you'll live.

— RONALD J. GLASSER, U.S. ARMY DOCTOR

.   .   .

The training and dedication of the doctors, nurses, and
medics who cared for their wounded comrades played a

vital role as well. Medical miracles were performed daily.

Medics were almost universally referred to as "Doc." Their job was to keep the wounded alive until they could be med-evac-ed out. Being a medic was particularly dangerous. Like officers, they were shot at first by the enemy. During one particularly bloody battle ten medics were killed and five seriously injured in the first five hours of the clash. Like the nurses, doctors, and surgeons, they learned to improvise.

• • •

> I learned that you can save a man's life with what he has on his person; you don't need a first-aid kit to save him. It's nice to have a first-aid kit because you have an airway, morphine, tourni-quets and battle dressings. But you can stop bleeding with a belt, you can stop bleeding with a piece of string out of a poncho. You can tear a piece of clothing off a man for a battle dressing. You can stop a sucking chest wound with the cel-lophane off a cigarette pack. You can use his chin strap to secure things. I learned that first aid is a matter of primitive wits.
>
> — DOUGLAS ANDERSON, U.S. MARINES

• • •

They learned too that many of the things that they were taught back in the States just didn't make it in the bush.

• • •

> . . . not even working with earthquake victims or in the emergency room of a big hospital could equal what I saw in Vietnam.
>
> . . . There were belly wounds, amputations, head

injuries, burns. On top of that they all had infections and complications. They had things we'd never heard about in school — things some of the physicians had never even heard about — and diseases they told us people hardly ever got anymore. Dengue fever. Malaria. Hepatitis. Bubonic plague.

— RUTH SIDISIN, U.S. AIR FORCE NURSING CORPS

.   .   .

Nurses in triage divided the wounded into three groups: those who required immediate care; those who did not; and those who could not survive no matter what was done for them. Time, available personnel, equipment, the number of wounded being cared for, and the extent of an individual's injuries were all taken into account in making this life/death decision.

.   .   .

It's another nurse, Grace, who first realizes the terrible truth. She's standing by his side, holding high a syringe with liquid food to pass through a tube into his stomach, when she sees his tears. Guessing but not wanting to believe, she asks him to blink. He does.

Grace tells him to blink twice, and he does. She tells him to shut his eyes, and he does — tears cascading down his cheeks for the joy of someone speaking to him.

He is fully alert but "locked in," paralyzed from the eyes down from a severed brainstem. He is able only to blink, move his eyes up and down, and cry, and there's no hope of his ever doing more than that. . . .

We print the alphabet on a piece of cardboard, so he can communicate more than yes or no. We run a finger along the letters, and he blinks out a message.

Once in the middle of a quiet night he blinks the message "L-E-T M-E D-I-E.". . .

— WINNIE SMITH, U.S. ARMY NURSE

.   .   .

Medical personnel — doctors, surgeons, nurses, corpsmen — worked around the clock when necessary. They learned to keep their emotions a safe distance away in order to perform their job properly. They hardened themselves to their surroundings in order to save lives.

.   .   .

I remember the first guy I treated. A young guy, about eighteen or nineteen. He had stepped on a Bouncing Betty, and it literally blew him apart. I remember running up and him saying, "Doc, Doc, I'm going to live, ain't I?" And me saying, "Sure, babe," and then he died. I held his hand, and he died. I remember crying. I cried at the next one and cried at the next one and cried at the next one. But it got to a point where I stopped crying, because I thought I'd either kill myself or go crazy if I felt for these guys. I started thinking, I'm going to stand up next time in a firefight and expose myself and end it. So I started shutting down. Not having any emotions. Steeling myself: You've gotta make it, therefore you can't cry anymore. I put myself in a cage. It worked enough that I could function. . . .

After a while it became a job. It became like factory work. Okay, he's hurt — treat him. Go to the next, treat him. Don't feel — move. Don't feel — move. One thing I started doing was not asking guys their names when they came into the company. Eventually I'd learn them, but I didn't want to know. They were humans but I didn't want them to be humans I knew. I didn't want to hear about their families. I didn't want to know where they were from . . . my attitude was: You get hurt, I'll treat you. That's it. Don't talk to me. Just don't talk to me.

— JACK MCCLOSKEY, U.S. MARINES

. . .

At times the pressure was unbearable. Something had to give and sometimes people were changed forever.

. . .

. . . I had lost it. I screamed and ran out the door. I remember screaming at the top of my lungs — all kinds of obscenities. And I remember being outside and there were helicopters going out on a mission and I was yelling "Kill, kill, kill!" and all kinds of awful stuff. I just walked around the hospital in my OR clothes, screaming and crying. I had lost it. No self-control at all . . . in all honesty I don't remember a thing after that. The whole thing is gone. The only thing I remember is being in the chief nurse's

office, yelling at her to get me out of there. I told
her please to let me work in the malaria ward. The
next thing I remember, I was on R and R.

So I laid on the beach in the sun for three days.
I ate pineapples. And when I got back to Cu Chi,
I'd built a wall that nothing or nobody was going
to get through. I was different now. I was bitter.
And I remembered how when I'd first gotten to
Vietnam I'd met a lot of doctors that seemed cyni-
cal. At the time I hadn't understood it. But now I
was just like they were. . . .

— SARALEE MCGORAN, U.S. ARMY NURSE

. . .

Facilities and equipment varied. There were fully
equipped hospitals in the base areas and field hospitals —
tents — set up on the periphery of battle. At times some
emergency rooms lacked running water and electricity.
The medical staff learned to adapt. They realized that many
of the standards followed in the States just wouldn't work
in Vietnam. They learned to work with what they had.

American soldiers were given medical attention first.
Soldiers of the South Vietnamese army were routinely
treated last. The wounded enemy presented a more complicated problem.

. . .

In the recovery room, my first assignment was
a POW. When this male nurse told me, I told him
to shove it — I was not going to take care of any
North Vietnamese. But this nurse said, "Let me
tell you some things. First, I know how you feel

— none of us wants to take care of the enemy. Second, these people have a lot of information. We know they're upper rank. You may end up saving one hundred GIs — so just think of it that way." And I said, "OK — you're on."

— LILY ADAMS, U.S. ARMY NURSE

•   •   •

And there were times when caring for the wounded revealed the unspeakable futility and horror of war in a way that nothing else could.

•   •   •

The guy who sticks in my mind the most, he got hit with . . . a rocket-propelled grenade. . . . It blew off one leg at the thigh and one leg at the ankle. It took off his left arm at the shoulder, took off the tips of all his fingers on the other hand . . . He was what you'd call a real basket case. When he came in we were all going crazy because he was bleeding all over the place and nobody thought he was going to live. Somebody put pneumatic tourniquets on both his legs, the kind you inflate, and I was trying to hold him up while they put a clean sheet on the operating table because it was all blood-soaked. Well, somebody else turned the tourniquets on before the guy was asleep. The guy reached up with his only hand that had the fingers blown off and he grabbed me by the face, because he was in so much pain that he was grabbing out for something. He was screaming bloody murder and I was screaming bloody murder because his finger bones were sticking right in my skin. Everybody was yelling and screaming, trying to get this guy intubated and put to sleep. But there was no place to stick IVs in him. Every place that you'd normally put an IV in was gone. And he was bleeding to death. The only thing they could do was vein cutdowns on his neck to stick the blood right into his neck. Later on I had to do the leg that was blown off at the thigh. I remember grabbing those big muscles of the leg and pulling them back, and there were rocks . . . and tree branches. I thought, "Holy Christ, no wonder the guy went crazy when they turned on that tourniquet." I'd pick up one great big muscle and pull it back and try to dig out as much of the dirt as I could. Everybody was expecting the guy to die and half figuring that it would be better. Sure as hell, the guy lived through it. The next day I saw him over in the recovery room, and he was real happy about it. "Oh boy, I'm alive."

— JAMES HAGENZIEKER, U.S. ARMY

• • •

Vets

I had been in California for about a month when one day there was a big photo on the front page of the *L.A. Times* — a group of vets had gone to Washington and thrown away their medals. It was one of the most moving antiwar demonstrations there had been. I would have given anything to have been there with them. . . . Suddenly I knew my easy life could never be enough for me. The war had not ended. It was time for me to join forces with other vets.

— RON KOVIC, U.S. MARINES

. . .

Over 2.5 million Americans had served in Vietnam. Nearly one million saw combat. They were younger — on average, seven years younger — than their fathers who had fought in World War II. An unusually high number were physically and mentally crippled by the war. The transition from battlefield to hometown was rapid and rocky. Many were unable to leave the war behind.

. . .

You know, you begin to see a lot of instant insanity and brutality that I don't think anybody prepared you for, and then one day, all of a sudden, you're back on this airplane, with stewardesses and people who are laughing and happy — and you're coming out of this freaky atmosphere, and you land back in the United States of America. And nobody cares, and nobody wants you to be in uniform. You get in a taxi and off you go! You try to go home.

— JOHN KERRY, U.S. NAVY

. . .

There were no ticker-tape parades, motorcades, no keys to the city offered by the mayor. They were greeted, in many cases, with indifference and hostility. Some people at home didn't even know they had been away. Others did, but didn't want to hear what it was like.

. . .

. . . The people who had been my closest friends really knew nothing about Vietnam. They were only interested in what the war was like in terms of their preconceptions of what war was about: "How many people did you kill?" That kind of thing. Not really interested in the intense experiences we'd undergone, and how they might affect somebody. . . .

— JAMES HEBRON, U.S. MARINES

. . .

They had fought in a war that America was losing. Back home people preferred to ignore them, but they were hard to ignore.

The media pictured them as unstable and prone to violence, imagining that they were still in a firefight, back in "Nam." They were ticking bombs, waiting to explode. And, indeed, many were.

. . .

After I got out of the military . . .

And I was angry all the time. I don't even know why I was so angry . . . I carried around that anger like a fifty-pound bag of shit on my back. I used it as a reason for drinking, as a reason for my marriage breaking up. . . .

. . . I was getting thoughts like, "I'd be better off dead.". . . I never got violent or anything, but it was there. I knew it was only a matter of time before it came out. . . .

— WOODY WANAMAKER, U.S. ARMY

. . .

Hundreds of thousands of the vets were believed to be suffering from what would come to be called Post-Traumatic Stress Disorder. In previous wars this condition was called "shell shock" or "battle fatigue." Its symptoms — anxiety, depression, panic, and violence — could occur five, ten, or fifteen years later.

Others came home as addicts: marijuana, cocaine, heroin, alcohol.

Suicide rates were high and depression was commonplace.

They were alienated from the rest of their generation — those who had continued their education or entered the job market while they were off fighting on foreign soil, those who had already begun building their lives.

Vietnam veterans began to form a significant portion of the nation's unemployed. Some were told not to mention that they had been in Vietnam on their resumés and job applications. They might find it easier to find a job.

.   .   .

> . . . this guy was telling me that he . . . wouldn't hire a Vietnam vet. . . . I was sort of dumbfounded by this. It's a classic case of blaming the warrior for the war. I was offended by that. He thought we were all crazy.
>
> — JAMES HEBRON, U.S. MARINES

.   .   .

They were considered outcasts, people to be avoided.

There were articles in magazines with titles like, "How to Treat a Viet Vet," and advice from a variety of "experts."

Many found the transition from the electrically charged

life of war in Vietnam to the quiet pace of normal life hard, and in some cases impossible, to adjust to.

Some came home deeply disturbed by the guilt they felt for having fought and killed in Vietnam. The antiwar atmosphere troubled some, angered others.

• • •

We would see all the stuff on the news at night. A village after we'd gone through it. They'd show a bunch of Vietnamese children in hospitals, all bandaged up, but they never showed a village after the VC went through it. They never took the cameras into the hospital wards and showed American GIs. What should have been said was, "End the war now, or declare war." One way or the other. That didn't happen, and they portrayed us as drug-crazed baby and women killers. When we got back, it was bad. . . . On any police program it was always a Vietnam vet flipping out and shooting people. Flashback to Vietnam: "He thinks he's in the war. Shoot him."

— DONALD HINES, U.S. MARINES

• • •

. . . Though our homes are safe from mortars and our countryside from snipers, controversy ranges over the war. It's the warmongers against the peaceniks. Caught in the middle are the returning warriors. Everyone is too busy taking sides or going on with his or her life . . .

When attention does focus on the soldiers, it's the wrong kind . . .

While I avoid discussing it, inside I scream. . . .
I'd like them to get off their self-righteous asses
and learn about war firsthand. I want them to be
terrified for their lives day in and day out, to
watch a couple of buddies get blown to pieces and
then see how long they can hang on to their high-
and-mighty ideals.
— WINNIE SMITH, U.S. ARMY NURSE

.   .   .

Many felt the government had betrayed them. They had
been sent thousands of miles from home, and then the
government did nothing to help them when they got back.
It was as if the government, like their neighbors, wanted to
make believe they didn't exist. It was as if the government,
like the population at large, was ashamed of them, wanted
to put the war behind them and make believe it hadn't
happened. They had laid their lives on the line for the
country. And now, somehow, they were the ones being
blamed for what went on there.

Some, eventually, were only able to talk to others who
had been there.

In 1967 six who came home formed the Vietnam Veterans Against the War (VVAW). Membership grew to several
thousand.

For five days in April 1971, VVAW demonstrated against
the war. Nearly 2,000 marched from the Lincoln Memorial
to Arlington Cemetery. They were led by vets on crutches
and confined to wheelchairs. They wore what was left of
their combat uniforms and were joined by the mothers of
sons who had died in Vietnam.

Some witnesses said the police guarding the way had tears in their eyes. There were no cries of "draft dodger" or "communist" and no boos or laughter as the Vietnam Veterans Against the War marched.

They lobbied Congress and listened to and testified at the hearings being held on the war.

.   .   .

> . . . we are told that the men who fought there must watch quietly while American lives are lost so that we can exercise the incredible arrogance of Vietnamizing the Vietnamese. Each day to facilitate the process by which the United States washes her hands of Vietnam someone has to give up his life so that the United States doesn't have to admit something that the entire world already knows, so that we can't say that we have made a mistake. Someone has to die so that President Nixon won't be, and these are his words, "The first President to lose a war."
>
> We are asking Americans to think about that because how do you ask a man to be the last man to die for a mistake?
>
> — JOHN KERRY, U.S. NAVY

.   .   .

They staged a sit-in on the steps of the Supreme Court and threw their medals and insignias of rank on the steps of the Capitol.

At one point during the five days of activities, a man wearing his dead son's fatigue jacket blew taps.

The wall

Dear Bill,

Today is February 13, 1984. I came to this black wall again to see and touch your name, and as I do I wonder if anyone ever stops to realize that next to your name on this black wall, is your mother's heart. A heart broken 15 years ago today, when you lost your life in Vietnam.

And as I look at your name, William R. Stocks, I think of how many, many times I used to wonder how scared and homesick you must have been in that strange country called Vietnam. And if and how it might have changed you, for you were the most happy-go-lucky kid in the world, hardly ever sad or unhappy . . .

Oh, God, how it hurts to write this. But I must face it and then put it to rest. . . .

They tell me the letters I write to you and leave here at this memorial are waking others up to the fact that there is still much pain left, after all these years, from the Vietnam War.

But this I know. I would rather to have had you for 21 years, and all the pain that goes with losing you, than never to have had you at all.

MOM

— MRS. ELEANOR WIMBISH, MOTHER OF
WILLIAM R. STOCKS, U.S. ARMY, KIA

chronology

111 B.C.	The beginning of recorded Vietnamese history and of a thousand years of Chinese rule.
Early 1500's	European colonial nations travel to Southeast Asia.
1883	A divided Vietnam comes under French control.
1890	Ho Chi Minh is born.
1914	World War I begins.
1918	World War I ends.
1930	Ho Chi Minh forms the Communist Party of Vietnam.
1939	World War II begins.
1941	Ho Chi Minh returns to Vietnam after thirty years in exile; forms the Vietminh.
1944	Vietminh army formed to fight the French.
1945	Franklin Delano Roosevelt dies; Harry S. Truman becomes president of the United States.
	Germany and Japan surrender — World War II ends.
	Ho Chi Minh declares the Democratic Republic of Vietnam — an independent nation.
1946	Vietminh attack the French after Haiphong is bombarded.
1948	Harry S. Truman elected 33rd president of the United States.
1949	Communist revolutionaries, led by Mao Zedong, come to power and proclaim the establishment of the People's Republic of China.
1950	The People's Republic of China and the Soviet Union recognize the government formed by Ho Chi Minh.
	The United States recognizes the government in the south, headed by Bao Dai.
	The Korean War begins.
1952	Dwight David Eisenhower is elected 34th president of the United States.
1953	Korean War ends.
1954	Geneva Conference begins.

Vietminh defeat the French at Dienbienphu.

Ngo Dinh Diem named Prime Minister of South Vietnam.

Geneva Conference ends: cease-fire declared; Vietnam temporarily divided into north and south; nationwide elections called for.

1955 U.S. begins to send aid directly to South Vietnam's government.

Diem refuses to participate in nationwide election; proclaims the Republic of South Vietnam with himself as president.

1957 Diem visits U.S.

Communist guerrillas assassinate South Vietnamese officials as part of a program to disrupt the government.

1959 Two American military advisors are killed in the Vietnam War.

1960 John Fitzgerald Kennedy elected 35th president of the United States.

The National Liberation Front for South Vietnam is formed by communists.

1961 Vice-President Lyndon Baines Johnson sent to South Vietnam.

1962 Diem's presidential palace bombed by South Vietnamese army pilots who oppose his rule.

1963 Buddhist demonstrations begin; martial law is declared.

Diem and his brother Ngo Dinh Nhu are killed during a military coup.

President Kennedy is assassinated; Lyndon Baines Johnson becomes president of the United States.

1964 General William Westmoreland takes over Military Assistance Command–Vietnam: (MACV).

The Tonkin Gulf incident occurs; Congress passes Tonkin Gulf Resolution.

Lyndon Baines Johnson elected 36th president of the United States.

1965 Operation Rolling Thunder begins.

The first U.S. combat troops — 3,500 Marines — arrive in Vietnam.

The first large antiwar demonstrations in the United States take place.

1966	American prisoners of war are paraded through the streets of Hanoi.
1967	Large antiwar demonstrations in Washington, D.C.
1968	The siege of Khe Sanh begins.
	Communists launch the Tet offensive.
	Senator Eugene McCarthy nearly defeats Lyndon Johnson in the New Hampshire primary.
	My Lai massacre occurs.
	President Johnson announces he will not seek reelection.
	The siege of Khe Sanh ends.
	Rev. Dr. Martin Luther King, Jr., is assassinated.
	The Paris Peace Talks begin.
	Senator Robert Kennedy is assassinated.
	General Creighton Abrams replaces Westmoreland.
	The Democratic National Convention is held in Chicago.
	President Johnson announces a halt to all bombing of North Vietnam.
	Richard Milhous Nixon is elected the 37th president of the United States.
1969	Operation Menu — the secret bombing of Cambodia — begins.
	President Nixon announces first U.S. troop withdrawals.
	U.S. and North Vietnamese meet in secret negotiating sessions.
	Ho Chi Minh dies.
	Large antiwar demonstrations occur in Washington, D.C., and other cities.
1970	U.S. and South Vietnamese forces invade Cambodia.
	Four Kent State University students are killed by national guardsmen; 400 college campuses are shut down as a result of protest.
	The trial of Lieutenant Calley for the massacre at My Lai begins.
1971	Lieutenant Calley is found guilty of premeditated murder.
	The New York Times begins publication of the Pentagon Papers.

1972 President Nixon visits China and the Soviet Union.
The Watergate break-in occurs.
President Nixon is re-elected.
The Paris Peace Talks break down.
President Nixon orders "The Christmas Bombing" of
North Vietnam.

1973 A peace agreement is signed in Paris.
The last U.S. ground combat troops leave Vietnam.
American POWs are released.

1974 Fighting between North and South Vietnam resumes,
openly.
Richard Nixon resigns; Gerald R. Ford becomes the
38th president of the United States.

1975 The North Vietnamese begin their final offensive.
The South Vietnamese army retreats in disarray and
disgrace; cities fall to the communists and panic
spreads.
President Thieu resigns and leaves the country.
All U.S. personnel are evacuated from Saigon.
Communist forces enter Saigon and the war is over.

gl●ssary

AGENT ORANGE
the defoliant used most often by the
United States (see DEFOLIATE)

AK-47
the standard assault rifle used by
the North Vietnamese Army and the
Vietcong

ANTIPERSONNEL MINES
explosive weapons designed to
injure or kill people rather than
damage or destroy things

**ARMORED PERSONNEL
CARRIERS (APCs)**
vehicles designed to transport infantry troops to the combat zone,
while protecting them from artillery
and small arms fire; they were also
adapted for use as assault vehicles

BLOODS
a term used by black soldiers to
describe themselves

BOOBY TRAPS
mines, grenades, other explosives,
and even simple mechanisms like
sharpened punji sticks, set, pointed
end up, in camouflaged holes

BOONIERAT
(see BOONIES)

BOONIES
the Vietnamese countryside;
"humping the boonies" meant
searching for the enemy, while
"boonierats" were the infantrymen
who did the searching

BOUNCING BETTY
(see ANTIPERSONNEL MINES)

CH-21
the "workhorse" helicopter used to
carry troops and cargo

CH-47 CHINOOK
a large, twin engine transport helicopter capable of carrying three
tons of supplies or thirty soldiers

CHARLIE
Vietcong guerrillas

CHERRIES
inexperienced soldiers

CHOPPER
helicopter

CLAYMORE
(see ANTIPERSONNEL MINES)

COUNTERINSURGENCY
a response to guerrilla wars involving a multifaceted approach, including: pacifying the civilian population; operating within the law; and supporting a stable and democratic government

COUP D'ÉTAT
the forceful takeover of a government by a small group

DEFOLIATE
the use of herbicides to destroy vegetation

DEMILITARIZED ZONE (DMZ)
the five-mile-wide area that separated North and South Vietnam

DOVES
anyone, especially public figures, who opposed the war

ELEPHANT GRASS
high, tropical grass with razor-sharp edges

FIRE BASE
a temporary installation that provides artillery support for units during ground operations

FIREFIGHT
a skirmish involving small arms fire

FLAK JACKET
a vest filled with fiberglass and worn during artillery attacks for protection from shrapnel wounds

GENEVA CONVENTIONS
a series of agreements named after international conferences that resulted in humanitarian laws governing the conduct of war — including the treatment of prisoners of war

GREAT SOCIETY
the name given to the domestic reforms promised by President Lyndon Johnson. He called for an end to poverty and racial injustice.

GUERRILLA WAR
unconventional warfare waged by irregular forces who are operating within their own country; they use ambushes, hit-and-run tactics, the destruction of lines of communications, constant harassment, and knowledge of the terrain, to offset their enemy's superiority in numbers and firepower (guerrilla means "little war" in Spanish)

HAMLET
a small, rural village

HAWKS
anyone, especially public figures, who supported the war

HERBICIDES
(see DEFOLIATE)

HUMPING
(see BOONIES)

IN COUNTRY
Vietnam; fighting in Vietnam

KIA
killed in action

LANDING ZONES (LZs)
a clearing where helicopters land
to deliver or pick up troops or
supplies

M-16
the standard infantry weapon used
by the U.S. military

NAPALM
short for *na*phthenic and *palm*itic
acids; a jellied gasoline that was
dropped from planes in large
canisters that exploded and
burned everything in the area

NVA
North Vietnamese Army

PEASANTS
poor farmers

PUNJI STICKS
sharpened bamboo sticks

ROTC
Reserve Officers' Training Corps

SAIGON
South Vietnam's capital during the
war

SELECTIVE SERVICE
the law that required men between
the ages of 18 and 26 to register for
military service

SHRAPNEL
metal pieces that result from an
explosion caused by a bomb or
artillery shell

SORTIE
a round-trip mission flown by a
single aircraft

STARLIGHT SCOPE
an instrument that provides night
vision

TEACH-INs
a form of protest against the war
that included speeches, seminars,
and informal discussions on university campuses

TRIAGE
dividing the wounded into groups
based on their condition: those who
need immediate care; those who
need minimal care; and those
who will not survive no matter
what care they are given

VC
Vietcong

THE WORLD
the United States

s●urce n●tes

p. xi   Michael Maclear, *The Ten Thousand Day War: Vietnam 1945–1975* (New York: St. Martin's Press, 1981), p. 318.

p. xv   Larry Rottmann, Jan Barry, and Basil T. Paquet, eds., *Winning Hearts and Minds: War Poems by Vietnam Veterans* (New York: McGraw Hill Book Company, 1972), p. 9.

Chapter One: The Dirty War

p. 3   Harry Maurer, *Strange Ground: Americans in Vietnam 1945–1975: An Oral History* (New York: Henry Holt and Company, 1989), p. 45.

p. 3   David Chanoff and Doan Van Thoi, *Portrait of the Enemy: The Other Side of the War in Vietnam, Told Through Interviews with North Vietnamese, Former Vietcong and Southern Opposition Leaders* (New York: Random House, 1986), pp. 58–59.

Chapter Two: The Miracle Man

p. 5   Stanley Karnow, *Vietnam: A History* (New York: The Viking Press, 1984), p. 214.

p. 5   John S. Bowman, *The World Almanac of the Vietnam War* (New York: World Almanac, 1985), p. 35.

p. 6   George McT. Kahin, *Intervention: How America Became Involved in Vietnam* (New York: Alfred A. Knopf, 1986), p. 81.

pp. 6–7 John Mecklin, *Mission in Torment: An Intimate Account of the U.S. Role In Vietnam* (Garden City, N.Y.: Doubleday & Company, Inc., 1965), p. 40.

p. 7   Al Santoli, *Everything We Had: An Oral History of the Vietnam War by 33 Americans Who Fought It* (New York: Random House, 1981), p. 10.

p. 8   Truong Nhu Tang, *A Vietcong Memoir: An Inside Account of the Vietnam War and Its Aftermath* (New York: Vintage Books, 1986), p. 38.

        Al Santoli, *To Bear Any Burden: The Vietnam War and Its After-*

math in the Words of Americans and Southeast Asians (New York: E.P. Dutton, Inc., 1985), p. 76.

Chapter Three: Bear Any Burden

p. 9   Santoli, To Bear Any Burden, p. ix.

pp. 9–10   Maurer, pp. 85, 89.

p. 11   Rick Atkinson, The Long Gray Line: The American Journey of West Point's Class of 1966 (Boston: Houghton Mifflin Company, 1989), p. 22.

pp. 11–12   Theodore C. Sorensen, Kennedy (New York: Harper & Row, Publishers, 1965), pp. 632–633.

p. 12   Maclear, p. 71.

p. 13   Santoli, Everything We Had, pp. 201–202.

p. 14   Bowman, p. 55.

p. 15   David Halberstam, The Best and the Brightest (New York: Random House, 1969), p. 175.

pp. 15–16   Maurer, p. 97.

p. 16   Santoli, Everything We Had, p. 7.

pp. 16–17   Mecklin, p. 156.

p. 17   Judith Vecchione, writer and producer, Vietnam: A Television History (WGBH, Boston; Central Independent Television, UK; Antennae-2, France, in association with LRE Productions—1983 WGBH Educational Foundations), (103–15)
              Mecklin, p. 178.
              Gary R. Hess, Vietnam and the United States: Origins and Legacy of War (Boston: Twayne Publishers, 1990), p. 76.

p. 18   Vietnam: A Television History (103–15)

p. 19   Bowman, pp. 48–49.

p. 19   Ellen J. Hammer, A Death in November: America in Vietnam, 1963 (New York: E.P. Dutton, 1987), p. 198.

p. 19   Vietnam: A Television History (103–16)

pp. 19–20   Ibid., (103–18)

p. 20   Hammer, p. 285.

pp. 20–21   Halberstam, p. 264.
              Vietnam: A Television History (103–19)

p. 21   Marguerite Higgins, Our Vietnam Nightmare (New York: Harper & Row, Publishers, 1965), p. 215.

p. 22   Hammer, p. 83.

Chapter Four: The Tonkin Gulf Incident

p. 25   Halberstam, p. 414.

pp. 25–26   *The New York Times, The Pentagon Papers* (New York: Quad-
            rangle Books, 1971), pp. 133–134.

p. 26   Halberstam, p. 298.

pp. 26–27   Santoli, *To Bear Any Burden*, p. 3.

p. 27   Maclear, p. 144.

p. 27   Kahin, p. 183.

p. 28   James William Gibson, *The Perfect War: The War We Couldn't
            Lose and How We Did* (New York: Vintage Books, 1988),
            p. 81.

pp. 29–30   Karnow, p. 372.

p. 30   *Times*, pp. 272–273.

p. 31   Kahin, p. 221.

pp. 31–32   *Vietnam: A Television History* (104–7)

pp. 32–33   Karnow, p. 372.

Chapter Five: Rolling Thunder

p. 34   Neil Sheehan, *A Bright Shining Lie: John Paul Vann and
            America in Vietnam* (New York: Random House, 1988),
            p. 380.

pp. 34–35   Maurer, pp. 374, 376–377.

p. 36   *Vietnam: A Television History* (105–15)

p. 36   Maurer, p. 383.

pp. 36–37   Karnow, p. 458.

pp. 37–38   Maurer, p. 382.

p. 38   *Vietnam: A Television History* (104–13)

p. 38   Maurer, pp. 453–454.

p. 39   Karnow, pp. 458–459.

p. 39   *Vietnam: A Television History* (106–15)

p. 41   Karnow, p. 498.
            Ibid, p. 454.

p. 41   Bowman, p. 131.

p. 41   Townsend Hoopes, *The Limits of Intervention* (New York:
            W.W. Norton & Company, 1987), p. 185.

Chapter Six: "In Country"

p. 45   Sheehan, p. 526.

p. 45   Halberstam, p. 572.

p. 45   Santoli, *To Bear Any Burden*, p. 101.

p. 46   *Vietnam: A Television History* (104–13)

p. 47   Maclear, p. 155.

p. 47   *Vietnam: A Television History* (104–15)

p. 48   Kathryn Marshall, *In the Combat Zone: Vivid Personal Recollections of the Vietnam War from the Women Who Served There* (New York: Penguin Books, 1987), p. 84.

p. 48   *Vietnam: A Television History* (105–11)

pp. 48–49   Bernard Edelman, ed., *Dear America: Letters Home from Vietnam* (New York: W.W. Norton & Company, 1985), pp. 205–206.

pp. 49–50   *Vietnam: A Television History* (105–12)

p. 50   Heather Brandon, *Casualties: Death in Vietnam; Anguish and Survival in America* (New York: St. Martin's Press, 1984), p. 103.

pp. 50–51   Edelman, pp. 36–37.

pp. 51–52   Marshall, pp. 37–40.

p. 52   Ibid., p. 118.

pp. 52–53   Santoli, *Everything We Had*, pp. 34–35.

p. 53   Maurer, p. 176.

pp. 53–54   Santoli, *Everything We Had*, p. 71.

p. 54   Ibid., p. 64.

pp. 54–55   *Vietnam: A Television History* (105–15)

p. 55   Brandon, p. 179.

p. 55   Maurer, p. 112.

pp. 55–56   Wallace Terry, *Bloods: An Oral History of the Vietnam War by Black Veterans* (New York: Random House, 1984), pp. 16–17.

pp. 56–57   Santoli, *Everything We Had*, p. 3.

Chapter Seven: Winning Hearts and Minds

p. 58   Jonathan Schell, *The Village of Ben Suc* (New York: Alfred A. Knopf, 1967), p. 97.

pp. 58–59   Santoli, *Everything We Had*, p. 35.

p. 59   Maurer, p. 326.

pp. 59–60   Santoli, *Everything We Had*, p. 48.

p. 60   Schell, p. 13.

pp. 60–61   Karnow, pp. 467–468.

p. 61   Marilyn B. Young, *The Vietnam Wars: 1945–1990* (New York:
             HarperCollins Publishers, 1991), p. 144.

pp. 61–62   Santoli, *To Bear Any Burden*, p. 88.

pp. 62–64   Le Ly Hayslip, with Jay Wurts, *When Heaven and Earth
             Changed Places: A Vietnamese Woman's Journey from War to
             Peace* (New York: Doubleday, 1989), pp. 42–44.

Chapter Eight: ARVN

p. 65   Karnow, p. 500.

p. 65   Ibid., p. 262.

pp. 65–66   *Vietnam: A Television History* (104–12)

pp. 67–68   Mecklin, p. 62.
             Ibid, p. 94.

pp. 68–69   *Vietnam: A Television History* (105–13)

p. 69   Santoli, *To Bear Any Burden*, p. 99.

p. 69   Maurer, p. 524.

Chapter Nine: Guerilla War

p. 70   Douglas Pike, *Viet Cong: The Organization and Techniques of
             the National Liberation Front of South Vietnam* (Cambridge,
             Mass.: The MIT Press, 1966), p. 34.

p. 70   Ibid., p. 35.
             Sorensen, p. 632.

p. 71   Myra MacPherson, *Long Time Passing: Vietnam and the
             Haunted Generation* (Garden City, N.Y.: Doubleday &
             Company, Inc., 1984), p. 177.

pp. 71–72   Eric M. Bergerud, *The Dynamics of Defeat: The Vietnam War in
             Hau Nghia Province* (Boulder: Westview Press, 1991),
             p. 229.

p. 72   Santoli, *Everything We Had*, pp. 68–69.

p. 72   Santoli, *To Bear Any Burden*, p. 90.

pp. 72–73   Karnow, p. 467.

p. 73   Marshall, p. 131.

p. 74   Hayslip, with Wurts, p. 72.

p. 74   Terry, p. 114.

p. 75   Karnow, p. 470.

p. 75   Santoli, *Everything We Had*, p. 23.

pp. 75–76   Maurer, p. 276.

pp. 76–77   Terry, pp. 21–22.

pp. 77–78   John Sack, *Lieutenant Calley: His Own Story* (New York: The Viking Press, 1970), pp. 42–43.

p. 78   Terry, p. 96.

pp. 78–79   Maurer, pp. 165–166.

p. 79   Santoli, *Everything We Had*, p. 69.

pp. 79–80   Maurer, p. 196.

p. 80   Karnow, p. 472.

pp. 80–81   *Vietnam: A Television History* (105–7)

Chapter Ten: Search and Destroy

p. 82   Maclear, p. 189.
             Maurer, p. 450.

p. 83   Karnow, p. 422.

p. 83   Ibid., p. 426.

p. 84   Hess, p. 95.

p. 84   Maurer, p. 143.

pp. 84–85   Sheehan, p. 584.

p. 85   Maurer, p. 211.

p. 85   Schell, p. 20.

p. 86   Hoopes, p. 51.

p. 86   *Vietnam: A Television History* (105–9)

p. 88   Marshall, pp. 212–213.

p. 89   Santoli, *Everything We Had*, p. 26.

pp. 89–90   Ibid., pp. 36–37.

p. 90   Sheehan, p. 573

p. 91   Karnow, p. 406.

p. 92   Don Oberdorfer, *Tet!* (New York: Da Capo Press, 1971), p. 50.
             Halberstam, p. 665.

Chapter Eleven: Body Count

p. 93   Edelman, p. 103.

p. 94   Maclear, p. 199.

p. 94   Santoli, *Everything We Had*, p. 85.

p. 95   Gibson, p. 120.

pp. 95–96   Ibid., pp. 125–126.

pp. 96–97   Brandon, p. 110.

p. 97   Gibson, p. 127.

p. 97   Maurer, p. 195.
p. 98   Terry, p. 23.
p. 98   Karnow, p. 469.
pp. 98–99   David Halberstam, *The Making of a Quagmire* (New York: Random House, 1964), p. 85.
p. 99   *Vietnam: A Television History* (105–12)
pp. 99–100   Young, p. 165.
p. 100   *Vietnam: A Television History* (105–12)
p. 101   Gibson, p. 162.
p. 101   Karnow, p. 512.
p. 102   Edelman, p. 199.

Chapter Twelve: The War at Home

p. 103   Charles De Benedetti and Charles Chatfield, assisting author, *An American Ordeal: The Anti-war Movement of the Vietnam Era* (Syracuse: Syracuse University Press, 1990), p. 204.
p. 105   *Vietnam: A Television History* (111–14)
p. 106   De Benedetti and Chatfield, p. 158.
p. 108   Edelman, p. 205.
pp. 108–109 Ibid., p. 212.
p. 109   Ibid., pp. 209–211.
pp. 109–110 Santoli, *Everything We Had*, pp. 47–48.
pp. 110–111 Edelman, pp. 118–119.
pp. 111–112 Santoli, *To Bear Any Burden*, p. 111.

Chapter Thirteen: Tet

p. 115   *Vietnam: A Television History* (107–11)
p. 115   Oberdorfer, p. 2.
pp. 116–117 Santoli, *To Bear Any Burden*, pp. 183–184.
p. 117   Ibid., p. 184.
pp. 117–118 Ibid., p. 184.
p. 118   Brandon, p. 120.
p. 119   Frank Snepp, *Decent Interval: An Insider's Account of Saigon's Indecent End Told by the CIA's Chief Strategy Analyst in Vietnam* (New York: Random House, 1977), p. 13.
p. 119   Gibson, p. 165.
p. 120   Karnow, p. 532.
p. 121   Santoli, *Everything We Had*, pp. 111, 114–115.

p. 122   Karnow, p. 545.
p. 123   Oberdorfer, p. 158.
p. 124   Ibid., p. 249.
p. 124   Ibid., p. 250.
pp. 124–125   Santoli, *To Bear Any Burden*, p. 189.
p. 125   Ibid., p. 175.

Chapter Fourteen: Khe Sanh

p. 127   General William C. Westmoreland, *A Soldier Reports*
                (New York: Da Capo Press, 1989), p. 335.
p. 127   John Prados and Ray W. Stubbe, *Valley of Decision: The
                Siege of Khe Sanh* (Boston: Houghton Mifflin Com-
                pany, 1991), p. 191.
p. 128   Eric Hammel, *Khe Sanh: Siege in the Clouds—An Oral History*
                (New York: Crown Publishers, Inc., 1989), pp. 12–13.
p. 129   Prados and Stubbe, p. 351.
p. 130   Hammel, p. 95.
pp. 130–131   Edelman, pp. 80–81.
p. 131   Ibid., pp. 79–80.
p. 132   Ibid., pp. 83–84.
p. 132   Prados and Stubbe, pp. 8–9.
p. 133   Ibid., p. 286.
pp. 133–134   Hammel, pp. 178–179.
p. 134   Ibid., pp. 231–232.
pp. 135–136   Ibid., pp. 125–126.
p. 136   Prados and Stubbe, p. 307.
p. 137   Hammel, p. 252.
p. 138   Westmoreland, pp. 339–340.
pp. 139–141   Hammel, pp. 212–213.

Chapter Fifteen: The Whole World Is Watching

p. 143   Karnow, p. 479.
p. 143   Ibid., p. 481.
p. 144   Ibid., p. 555.
p. 145   *Vietnam: A Television History* (107–15)
p. 146   Oberdorfer, p. 177.
p. 148   Maclear, p. 259.

Chapter Sixteen: A Nightmare War

p. 155   Maclear, p. 317.

p. 156   Santoli, *Everything We Had*, p. 167.

p. 156   Maclear, p. 317.

p. 157   Maurer, p. 505.

p. 158   Santoli, *Everything We Had*, p. 95.

pp. 158–159   Maclear, p. 326.

pp. 159–160   Brandon, pp. 122–123.

p. 160   Karnow, p. 631.

pp. 160–161   *Vietnam: A Television History* (108–17)

p. 161   Santoli, *Everything We Had*, pp. 206–207.

p. 161   Terry, p. 40.

p. 162   *Vietnam: A Television History* (109–17)

p. 162   Santoli, *To Bear Any Burden*, p. 191.

p. 162   Maurer, p. 173.

pp. 163–164   Edelman, pp. 144–146.

pp. 164–165   Santoli, *To Bear Any Burden*, p. 190.

p. 165   Terry, p. 115.

pp. 165–166   *Vietnam: A Television History* (110–11)

p. 166   Michael Bilton and Kevin Sim, *Four Hours in My Lai* (New York: Viking, 1992), p. 1.

p. 167   Ibid., p. 98.

p. 167   Arthur Everett, Kathryn Johnson, and Harry F. Rosenthal, *Calley* (New York: Dell Publishing, 1971), p. 5.

p. 168   Seymour M. Hersh, *My Lai 4: A Report on the Massacre and Its Aftermath* (New York: Vintage Books, 1970), p. 51.

p. 168   Ibid., p. 91.

p. 169   Bilton and Sim, p. 335.

p. 170   Young, p. 256.

p. 170   Maurer, p. 357.

Chapter Seventeen: The Madman

p. 171   Karnow, p. 582.

p. 172   Santoli, *To Bear Any Burden*, p. 146.

p. 173   William Shawcross, *Sideshow: Kissinger, Nixon and the Destruction of Cambodia* (New York: Simon and Schuster, 1979), p. 22.

p. 174	Shawcross, p. 148.
	Vietnam: A Television History (109)
p. 175	Shawcross, p. 153.
p. 176	Karnow, p. 611.
p. 176	Nancy Zaroulis and Gerald Sullivan, *Who Spoke Up? American Protest Against the War in Vietnam 1963–1975* (Garden City, N.Y.: Doubleday & Company, Inc., 1984), p. 308.
p. 176	*Vietnam: A Television History* (110–111)
p. 176	Maclear, p. 341.
p. 178	Ibid., p. 362.
pp. 179–180	Santoli, *Everything We Had*, p. 223.
p. 181	Karnow, p. 623.
p. 183	Young, p. 294.
p. 184	Marshall, p. 82.

Chapter Eighteen: Coming Home

p. 187	Marshall, p. 40.
p. 187	Karnow, p. 373.
pp. 188–189	Santoli, *Everything We Had*, pp. 229–233.
p. 189	Terry, p. 139.
pp. 189–190	Santoli, *Everything We Had*, p. 234.
pp. 190–192	Ibid., pp. 237–240.
pp. 192–193	Maurer, p. 419.
p. 193	Ibid., p. 395.
p. 193	Ibid., pp. 419–420.
pp. 193–194	Ibid., p. 395.
p. 194	Santoli, *To Bear Any Burden*, p. 160.
p. 195	Christopher Andersen, *Citizen Jane: The Turbulent Life of Jane Fonda* (New York: Henry Holt and Company, 1990), p. 254.
pp. 195–196	Ibid., p. 255.
p. 196	Ibid., p. 258.
pp. 196–197	Maurer, p. 422.
p. 197	Santoli, *Everything We Had*, pp. 244–245.
pp. 198–199	Maurer, pp. 424–425.
p. 199	Edelman, pp. 75–76.
pp. 199–200	Santoli, *Everything We Had*, pp. 67–68, 75.
p. 200	Marshall, p. 198.

p. 201   Ronald J. Glasser, M.D., *365 Days* (New York: George
              Braziller, 1971), p. 8.
p. 202   Santoli, *Everything We Had*, p. 67.
pp. 202–203   Marshall, p. 29.
pp. 203–204   Winnie Smith, *American Daughter Gone to War* (New
              York: William Morrow and Company, Inc., 1992),
              p. 200.
pp. 204–205   Maurer, pp. 251, 254.
pp. 205–206   Marshall, pp. 250–251.
pp. 206–207   Ibid., p. 215.
pp. 207–208   Maurer, pp. 262–263.
pp. 208–209   Ron Kovic, *Born on the Fourth of July* (New York: Mc-
              Graw Hill Book Company, 1976), p. 133.
p. 209   *Vietnam: A Television History* (113–16)
p. 210   Brandon, p. 71.
p. 210   Maurer, pp. 247–248.
p. 211   Brandon, p. 86.
p. 212   Ibid., p. 143.
pp. 212–213   Smith, pp. 279–280.
p. 214   Zaroulis and Sullivan, p. 357.
p. 217   Edelman, pp. 299–300.

credits

Grateful acknowledgment is made to the following for granting permission to reprint copyrighted material:

From *American Daughter Gone to War: On the Front Lines with an Army Nurse in Vietnam*, by Winnie Smith. Copyright © 1992 by Winnie Smith. By permission of William Morrow and Company, Inc.

From *Bloods: An Oral History of the Vietnam War by Black Veterans*, by Wallace Terry. Copyright © 1984 by Wallace Terry. Reprinted by permission of Random House Inc.

From *Calley*, by Arthur Everett, Kathryn Johnson, and Harry F. Rosenthal. Copyright © 1971 by Arthur Everett, Kathryn Johnson, and Harry F. Rosenthal. Reprinted by permission of Dell Publishing, a division of Bantam Doubleday Dell Publishing Group, Inc.

From *Casualties: Death in Vietnam*, by Heather Brandon. Copyright © 1984 by Heather Brandon. Reprinted by permission of St. Martin's Press Inc.

From *Citizen Jane: The Turbulent Life of Jane Fonda*, by Christopher Andersen. Copyright © 1990 by Christopher Andersen. Reprinted by permission of Henry Holt & Co Inc.

From *Dear America: Letters Home from Vietnam*, edited by Bernard Edelman. Copyright © 1985 by Bernard Edelman. Reprinted by permission of Bernard Edelman and W.W. Norton & Company.

From *Everything We Had: An Oral History of the Vietnam War by 33 Americans Who Fought It*, by Al Santoli. Copyright © 1981 by Al Santoli. Reprinted by permission of Random House Inc.

From *Four Hours in My Lai*, by Michael Bilton and Kevin Sim. Copyright ©

1992 by Michael Bilton and Kevin Sim. Reprinted by permission of Viking Penguin, a division of Penguin Books USA Inc.

From *In the Combat Zone*, by Kathryn Marshall. Copyright © 1987 by Kathryn Marshall. By permission of Little, Brown and Company.

From *Khe Sanh: Siege in the Clouds—An Oral History*, by Eric Hammel. Copyright © 1989 by Eric Hammel. Reprinted by permission of The Crown Publishing Group.

From *Mission in Torment: An Intimate Account of the U.S. Role in Vietnam*, by John Mecklin. Copyright © 1965 by John Mecklin. Reprinted by permission of Doubleday and Co. a division of Bantam Doubleday Dell Publishing Group, Inc.

From *My Lai 4: A Report on the Massacre and Its Aftermath*, by Seymour M. Hersh. Copyright © 1970 by Seymour M. Hersh. Reprinted by permission of Random House Inc.

From *The Perfect War: The War We Couldn't Lose*, by James William Gibson. Copyright © 1986 by James William Gibson. Used by permission of Grove/Atlantic Inc.

From *Strange Ground: Americans in Vietnam 1945–1975: An Oral History*, by Harry Maurer. Copyright © 1989 by Harry Maurer. Reprinted by permission of Henry Holt & Co Inc.

From *The Ten Thousand Day War: Vietnam 1945–1975*, by Michael Maclear. Copyright © 1981 by Michael Maclear. Reprinted by permission of St. Martin's Press Inc.

From *To Bear Any Burden*, by Al Santoli. Copyright © 1985 by Al Santoli. Used by permission of Dutton Signet, a division of Penguin Books USA Inc.

From *Vietnam: A History*, by Stanley Karnow. Copyright © 1983 by WGBH Educational Foundation and Stanley Karnow. Used by permission of Viking Penguin, a division of Penguin Books USA Inc.

From *Vietnam: A Television History*. Written and produced by Judith Vecchione. A co-production of WGBH, Boston; Central Independent Television, UK; Antennae-2, France, in association with LRE Productions. Copyright © 1983 WGBH Educational Foundation. Used by permission.

From *The Vietnam Wars: 1945–1990*, by Marilyn B. Young. Copyright © 1991 by Marilyn B. Young. Reprinted by permission of HarperCollins Publishers Inc.

From *When Heaven and Earth Changed Places*, by Le Ly Hayslip. Copyright © 1989 by Le Ly Hayslip and Charles Jay Wurts. Used by permission of Doubleday, a division of Bantam Doubleday Dell Publishing Group, Inc.

Poem by Larry Rottmann from *Winning Hearts and Minds: War Poems by Vietnam Veterans*, edited by Larry Rottmann, Jan Barry, and Basil T. Paquet. Copyright © 1972 by Larry Rottmann. Reprinted by permission.

bibliography

Andersen, Christopher. *Citizen Jane: The Turbulent Life of Jane Fonda*. New York: Henry Holt and Company, 1990.

Atkinson, Rick. *The Long Gray Line: The American Journey of West Point's Class of 1966*. Boston: Houghton Mifflin Company, 1989.

Becker, Elizabeth. *America's Vietnam War: A Narrative History*. New York: Clarion Books, 1992.

Bergerud, Eric M. *The Dynamics of Defeat: The Vietnam War in Hau Nghia Province*. Boulder: Westview Press, 1991.

———. *Red Thunder, Tropic Lightning: The World of a Combat Division in Vietnam*. Boulder: Westview Press, 1993.

Berman, Larry. *Lyndon Johnson's War: The Road to Stalemate in Vietnam*. New York: W. W. Norton & Company, 1989.

Bilton, Michael, and Kevin Sim. *Four Hours in My Lai*. New York: Viking, 1992.

Blum, John Morton. *Years of Discord: American Politics and Society, 1961–1974*. New York: W. W. Norton & Company, 1991.

Bowman, John S. *The World Almanac of the Vietnam War*. New York: World Almanac, 1985.

Bradlee, Benjamin C. *Conversations with Kennedy*. New York: W. W. Norton & Company, 1975.

Brandon, Heather. *Casualties: Death in Vietnam; Anguish and Survival in America*. New York: St. Martin's Press, 1984.

Broyles, William, Jr. *Brothers in Arms: A Journey from Peace to War.* New York: Alfred A. Knopf, 1986.

Bryan, C. D. B. *Friendly Fire.* New York: G. P. Putnam's Sons, 1976.

Burns, James MacGregor. *The Crosswinds of Freedom.* New York: Alfred A. Knopf, 1989.

Cameron, James. *Here Is Your Enemy: James Cameron's Complete Report from North Vietnam.* New York: Holt, Rinehart and Winston, 1965.

Camp, R. D., with Eric Hammel. *Lima–6: A Marine Company Commander in Vietnam June 1967–January 1968.* New York: Atheneum, 1989.

Caute, David. *The Year of the Barricades: A Journey Through 1968.* New York: Harper & Row, 1988.

Chanoff, David, and Doan Van Thoi. *Portrait of the Enemy: The Other Side of the War in Vietnam, Told Through Interviews with North Vietnamese, Former Vietcong and Southern Opposition Leaders.* New York, Random House, 1986.

Coldfelter, Mark. *The Limits of Air Power: The American Bombing of North Vietnam.* New York: The Free Press, 1989.

Colby, William, with James McCargar. *Lost Victory: A Firsthand Account of America's Sixteen-Year Involvement in Vietnam.* Chicago: Contemporary Books, 1984.

Corson, William R. *The Betrayal.* New York: W. W. Norton & Company, 1968.

De Benedetti, Charles, and Charles Chatfield, assisting author. *An American Ordeal: The Anti-war Movement of the Vietnam Era.* Syracuse: Syracuse University Press, 1990.

Dooley, Thomas A., M.D. *Deliver Us from Evil: The Fantastic Experiences of a Navy Doctor Among the Terrorized Vietnamese Victims of the Communists.* New York: Farrar, Straus and Cudahy, 1956.

———. *The Edge of Tomorrow.* New York: W. W. Norton & Company, 1985.

Edelman, Bernard, ed. *Dear America: Letters Home from Vietnam.* New York: W. W. Norton & Company, 1985.

Emerson, Gloria. *Winners & Losers: Battles, Retreats, Gains, Losses, and Ruins from the Vietnam War.* New York: W. W. Norton & Company, 1976.

Ethell, Jeffrey, and Alfred Price. *One Day in a Long War: May 10, 1972, Air War, North Vietnam.* New York: Random House, 1989.

Everett, Arthur, Kathryn Johnson, and Harry F. Rosenthal. *Calley.* New York: Dell Publishing, 1971.

Fall, Bernard B. *Street Without Joy.* New York: Schocken Books, 1961.

FitzGerald, Frances. *Fire in the Lake: The Vietnamese and the Americans in Vietnam.* Boston: Atlantic Monthly Press, 1972.

Gibson, James William. *The Perfect War: The War We Couldn't Lose and How We Did.* New York: Vintage Books, 1988.

Gitlin, Todd. *The Sixties: Years of Hope, Days of Rage.* New York: Bantam Books, 1987.

Glasser, Ronald J., M.D. *365 Days.* New York: George Braziller, 1971.

Goodwin, Doris Kearns. *Lyndon Johnson and the American Dream.* New York: St. Martin's Press, 1991.

Grant, Zalin. *Facing the Phoenix: The CIA and the Political Defeat of the United States in Vietnam.* New York: W. W. Norton & Company, 1991.

Greenhaw, Wayne. *The Making of a Hero: The Story of Lieut. William Calley Jr.* Louisville: Touchstone Publishing Company, 1971.

Halberstam, David. *The Best and the Brightest.* New York: Random House, 1969.

———. *The Making of a Quagmire.* New York: Random House, 1964.

Hammel, Eric. *Khe Sanh: Siege in the Clouds: An Oral History.* New York: Crown Publishers, Inc., 1989.

Hammer, Ellen J. *A Death in November: America in Vietnam, 1963.* New York: E. P. Dutton, 1987.

Hayslip, Le Ly, with Jay Wurts. *When Heaven and Earth Changed Places: A Vietnamese Woman's Journey from War to Peace.* New York: Doubleday, 1989.

Herr, Michael. *Dispatches.* New York: Alfred A. Knopf, 1977.

Hersh, Seymour M. *Cover-Up: The Army's Secret Investigation of the Massacre at My Lai 4.* New York: Random House, 1972.

———. *My Lai 4: A Report on the Massacre and Its Aftermath.* New York: Vintage Books, 1970.

———. *The Price of Power: Kissinger in the Nixon White House.* New York: Summit Books, 1983.

Hess, Gary R. *Vietnam and the United States: Origins and Legacy of War.* Boston: Twayne Publishers, 1990.

Hess, Martha. *Then the Americans Came: Voices from Vietnam.* New York: Four Walls Eight Windows, 1993.

Hickey, Gerald Cannon. *Village in Vietnam.* New Haven: Yale University Press, 1964.

Higgins, Marguerite. *Our Vietnam Nightmare.* New York: Harper & Row, Publishers, 1965.

Hoobler, Dorothey, and Thomas Hoobler. *Vietnam: Why We Fought: An Illustrated History.* New York: Alfred A. Knopf, 1990.

Hoopes, Townsend. *The Limits of Intervention.* New York: W. W. Norton & Company, 1987.

Hung, Nguyen Tien, and Jerrold L. Schecter. *The Palace File*. New York: Harper & Row, Publishers, 1986.

Kahin, George McT. *Intervention: How America Became Involved in Vietnam*. New York: Alfred A. Knopf, 1986.

Kahin, George McTurnan, and John W. Lewis. *The United States in Vietnam*. New York: Delta Books, 1967.

Karnow, Stanley. *Vietnam: A History*. New York: The Viking Press, 1984.

Kelly, Francis J. *The Green Berets in Vietnam, 1961–1971*. Washington: Brassey's (US), Inc., 1991.

Kolko, Gabriel. *Anatomy of a War: Vietnam, the United States and the Modern Historical Experience*. New York: Pantheon Books, 1985.

Kovic, Ron. *Born on the Fourth of July*. New York: McGraw-Hill Book Company, 1976.

Krepinevich, Andrew F., Jr. *The Army and Vietnam*. Baltimore: The Johns Hopkins University Press, 1986.

Kutler, Stanley I. *The Wars of Watergate: The Last Crises of Richard Nixon*. New York: Alfred A. Knopf, 1990.

Lacouture, Jean. *Ho Chi Minh: A Political Biography*. New York: Random House, 1968.

Lang, Daniel. *Casualties of War*. New York: McGraw-Hill Book Company, 1969.

Luttwak, Edward, and Stuart L. Koehl. *The Dictionary of Modern War*. New York: HarperCollins Publishers, 1991.

McCarthy, Mary. *Hanoi*. New York: Harcourt Brace & World, Inc., 1967.

———. *Vietnam*. New York: Harcourt Brace & World, Inc., 1967.

MacDonald, Peter. *Giap: The Victor in Vietnam.* New York: W. W. Norton & Company, 1993.

Maclear, Michael. *The Ten Thousand Day War: Vietnam 1945–1975.* New York: St. Martin's Press, 1981.

MacPherson, Myra. *Long Time Passing: Vietnam and The Haunted Generation.* Garden City, N.Y.: Doubleday & Company, Inc., 1984.

Marshall, Kathryn. *In The Combat Zone: Vivid Personal Recollections of the Vietnam War from the Women Who Served There.* New York: Penguin Books, 1987.

Mason, Robert. *Chickenhawk.* New York: The Viking Press, 1983.

Maurer, Harry. *Strange Ground: Americans in Vietnam 1945–1975: An Oral History.* New York: Henry Holt and Company, 1989.

Mecklin, John. *Mission in Torment: An Intimate Account of the U.S. Role in Vietnam.* Garden City, N.Y.: Doubleday & Company, Inc., 1965.

Newman, John M. *JFK and Vietnam: Deception, Intrigue and the Struggle for Power.* New York: Warner Books, 1992.

The New York Times. The Pentagon Papers. New York: Quadrangle Books, 1971.

Oberdorfer, Don. *Tet!* New York: Da Capo Press, 1971.

Olsen, James, ed. *Dictionary of the Vietnam War.* New York: Peter Bedrick Books, 1987.

Pike, Douglas. *Viet Cong: The Organization and Techniques of the National Liberation Front of South Vietnam.* Cambridge, Mass.: The MIT Press, 1966.

Pisor, Robert. *The End of the Line: The Siege of Khe Sanh.* New York: W. W. Norton & Company, 1982.

Prados, John, and Ray W. Stubbe. *Valley of Decision: The Siege of Khe Sanh.* Boston: Houghton Mifflin Company, 1991.

Rottmann, Larry, Jan Barry and Basil T. Paquet, eds. *Winning Hearts and Minds: War Poems by Vietnam Veterans.* New York: McGraw-Hill Book Company, 1972.

Sack, John. *Lieutenant Calley: His Own Story.* New York: The Viking Press, 1970.

Salisbury, Harrison. *Behind the Lines — Hanoi: December 23, 1966–January 7, 1967.* New York: Harper & Row, Publishers, 1967.

Santoli, Al. *Everything We Had: An Oral History of the Vietnam War by 33 Americans Who Fought It.* New York: Random House, 1981.

——— . *To Bear Any Burden: The Vietnam War and Its Aftermath in the Words of Americans and Southeast Asians.* New York: E. P. Dutton, Inc., 1985.

Schell, Jonathan. *The Military Half: An Account of the Destruction of Quang Ngai and Quang Tin.* New York: Alfred A. Knopf, 1968.

——— . *The Village of Ben Suc.* New York: Alfred A. Knopf, 1967.

Shaplen, Robert. *The Road from War: Vietnam 1965–1970.* New York: Harper & Row, Publishers, 1970.

——— . *Time Out of Hand: Revolution and Reaction in Southeast Asia.* New York: Harper & Row, Publishers, 1969.

Shawcross, William. *Sideshow: Kissinger, Nixon and the Destruction of Cambodia.* New York: Simon and Schuster, 1979.

Sheehan, Neil. *A Bright Shining Lie: John Paul Vann and America in Vietnam.* New York: Random House, 1988.

Sheehan, Susan. *Ten Vietnamese.* New York: Alfred A. Knopf, 1967.

Smith, Winnie. *American Daughter Gone to War: On the Front Lines with an Army Nurse in Vietnam.* New York: William Morrow and Company, Inc., 1992.

Snepp, Frank. *Decent Interval: An Insider's Account of Saigon's Indecent End Told by the CIA's Chief Strategy Analyst in Vietnam.* New York: Random House, 1977.

Sontag, Susan. *Trip to Hanoi.* New York: Farrar, Straus & Giroux, 1968.

Sorensen, Theodore C. *Kennedy.* New York: Harper & Row, Publishers, 1965.

Spector, Ronald H. *After Tet: The Bloodiest Year in Vietnam.* New York: The Free Press, 1993.

Stanton, Shelby L. *Green Berets at War: U.S. Army Special Forces in Southeast Asia 1956–1975.* Novato, Calif.: Presidio, 1985.

Summers, Harry G. *Vietnam War Almanac.* New York: Facts on File Publications, 1985.

Tang, Truong Nhu. *A Vietcong Memory: An Inside Account of the Vietnam War and Its Aftermath.* New York: Vintage Books, 1986.

Terry, Wallace. *Bloods: An Oral History of the Vietnam War by Black Veterans.* New York: Random House, 1984.

Todd, Oliver. *Cruel April: The Fall of Saigon.* New York: W. W. Norton & Company, 1987.

Van DeMark, Brian. *Into the Quagmire: Lyndon Johnson and the Escalation of the Vietnam War.* New York: Oxford University Press, 1991.

Warren, James A. *Portrait of a Tragedy: America and the Vietnam War.* New York: Lothrop, Lee & Shepard Books, 1990.

Westmoreland, General William C. *A Soldier Reports.* New York: Da Capo Press, 1989.

Willenson, Kim, with the Correspondents of *Newsweek. The Bad War: An Oral History of the Vietnam War.* New York: New American Library, 1987.

Wyatt, Clarence R. *Paper Soldiers: The American Press and the Vietnam War.* New York: W. W. Norton & Company, 1993.

Young, Marilyn B. *The Vietnam Wars: 1945–1990.* New York: HarperCollins Publishers, 1991.

Zaroulis, Nancy, and Gerald Sullivan. *Who Spoke Up? American Protest Against the War in Vietnam 1963–1975.* Garden City, N.Y.: Doubleday & Company, Inc., 1984.

Videos:
Dear America: HBO Video, The Couturie Company, 1987.

Vietnam: A Television History. Written and produced by Judith Vecchione. A coproduction of WGBH Boston with Central Independent Television, UK, Antennae-2, France, in association with LRE Productions — 1983 WGBH Educational Foundations.

Vietnam: The Ten Thousand Day War. Executive Producer: Michael Maclear; Writer: Peter Arnett. TDW Copyright Holding, 1980.

Barry Denenberg is a critically acclaimed author of non-fiction for young readers. *Voice of Youth Advocates* said of his most recent work, *The True Story of J. Edgar Hoover and the FBI*, "This is an extraordinary book; with it, Denenberg reaches the highest standards of excellence in nonfiction." Mr. Denenberg is also the author of *Nelson Mandela: "No Easy Walk to Freedom,"* *Stealing Home: The Story of Jackie Robinson*, and *John Fitzgerald Kennedy: America's 35th President*.

Barry Denenberg lives in Bedford, New York, with his wife and daughter.